Following Jesus As Pilgrims, Servants And Prophets In The Twenty First Century:

Letters To My Grandchildren

– MICHAEL P. HORNSBY-SMITH –

An environmentally friendly book printed and bound in England by
www.printondemand-worldwide.com

FSC Mixed Sources
Product group from well-managed forests, and other controlled sources
www.fsc.org Cert no. TT-COC-002641
© 1996 Forest Stewardship Council

PEFC Certified
This product is from sustainably managed forests and controlled sources
www.pefc.org
PEFC/16-33-415

This book is made entirely of chain-of-custody materials

FastPrint Publishing
www.fast-print.net/store.php

Following Jesus As Pilgrims, Servants And Prophets in the Twenty-First Century: Letters To My Grandchildren

A catalogue record for this book is available from the British Library

ISBN 978-178456-015-7

First published 2014 by
FASTPRINT PUBLISHING
Peterborough, England.

Contents

Preface

This book has had a rather chequered history in the making. It had its origins around 1992 when my late friend Dominic McDonnell and I planned to write a pastoral plan for the Catholic Church in England and Wales. Dominic brought a lifetime's experience in business to the project and draft chapters included 'The Strategic Goals of the Church' and 'Managerial Strategies' as well as 'The Stewardship of Material Resources.' He interviewed a number of diocesan financial officers in seeking to base our proposals in the realities of diocesan resources and management. For a number of reasons this project was never completed. I was busy completing a study of RENEW[1] and editing a book on changes in English Catholicism over the second half of the twentieth century.[2]

But Dominic's and my endeavours continued with the focus shifted to 'The Future of the Church' from a committed layperson's perspective in the new context of the twenty-first century. But, rather to my surprise, Dominic advised me first to record my autobiographical impressions

---

1 M.P.Hornsby-Smith, J. Fulton, and M.I. Norris, *The Politics of Spirituality*, Oxford: Clarendon, 1995.

2 M.P.Hornsby-Smith (ed.), *Catholics in England 1950-2000*, London: Cassell, 1999.

and experiences in a wide range of Catholic organisations over the second half of the twentieth century. This was duly published in 2009.[3] Sadly Dominic died before we returned to consider the future of the Church.

The focus of this book changed yet again when the late Mildred Nevile, the former General Secretary of the Catholic Institute for International Relations (now Progressio) shared ideas at a lunch in October 2009. She challenged me in two ways in particular. First of all, instead of writing a book on *The Future of the Church* the focus should shift to what sort of life Catholic Christians should be living in the twenty-first century. In other words the focus should shift from the institutional Church to the ways which ordinary Catholics should aim to live as followers of Jesus in a sometimes aggressively secular world over the next few decades. How should my grandchildren live as pilgrim members of a servant Church in a hostile and unsympathetic world? Hence the shift to the title *Following Jesus as Pilgrims, Servants and Prophets in the Twenty First Century.*

The second challenge that Mildred made was to draw attention to the rapid social, economic and political changes of recent decades. In particular we were aware of significant generational changes and that my grandchildren are products of the internet age, ubiquitous mobile phones, ipads and other gadgets, Facebook, Twitter, YouTube and other social media. We noted that the most recent generations have never been trained to 'defer gratification' and save. Rather they had been encouraged to live on credit and spend beyond their means. They were influenced by a celebrity culture and were inclined to believe whatever they read on social network media. Whereas laity in the 1960s had been 'docile, deferential, respectful and submissive' towards priests, this was no longer the case.

---

3 M.P.Hornsby-Smith, *Reflections on a Catholic Life*, Peterborough: Fastprint, 2009.

In this book I have had my own grandchildren very much in mind as I have attempted to address the nature of the Catholic lay vocation in the twenty-first century. After a brief introductory chapter I have followed the well-known four-stage pastoral cycle. Thus Part I attempts to offer a sketch of the *social realities* of the world as it is emerging in the second decade of the twenty-first century including not only the over-riding reality of globalisation but also the insecure everyday world experienced by young people today. Part II will offer a *social analysis* of these social, economic, cultural and political trends and realities in terms of differential power relationships, the dominance of liberal capitalism and the countervailing forces generated by a growing awareness of global interdependence. Part III will suggest a *theological or religious framework* for critiquing the social realities from the perspectives of faith and necessitating a Church which is both servant and prophet. Finally, Part IV will propose some Christian responses and *social action* imperatives to the needs of the times arising out of the earlier analyses, addressed to followers of Jesus. There are thus nine chapters which can be regarded as nine letters to grandchildren and to young people generally. I have in mind in particular sixth formers, students and young people in their twenties struggling to become established in a preferred occupation, to get into the housing market, and to develop loving relationships and family life.

Many people over the years have contributed to the ideas which have been expressed in this book. In the first place I would like to thank both Dominic McDonnell and Mildred Nevile, both now with the Lord, for their gentle encouragement in the earlier stages of planning this project. David Beresford and John Williams kindly read draft chapters and advised me on how best to address sixth formers and young adults. Patrick Jordan helpfully suggested blogging possibilities. Bob Dixon, Director of the Pastoral Research Office of the Australian Bishops' Conference, kindly drew my attention to the wonderfully accessible book on *Social Justice*[4] written for Australian young people by Fr. Bruce Duncan. Kate Brett, editor of my earlier book at Cambridge University Press, also gave me helpful advice and encouragement. My thanks are also due to Pauline Tebbutt at Print on Demand. I am grateful to all of them for their patient advice and help.

I had in mind Bruce Duncan's book when revising the earlier draft of these letters. Thus while what I have written pays particular attention to the specific situation in the United Kingdom in the second decade of the twenty first century, I hope that it will also have resonances with young people elsewhere, particularly Australia, New Zealand and the United States. I hope that what I have written is reasonably accessible and challenging to sixth formers or older students and their Religious Education teachers, undergraduates and young Christians generally and that it might inspire them to take seriously the call to seek the kingdom of God here on earth through systematic and persistent justice-seeking.

As always my greatest debt is to my wife, Lennie, who has provided unstinting support for over half a century. Without her tolerance and generosity I would never have finished this project.

I dedicate this book to my six grandchildren Luke, Benedict, Katie, Douglas, Will and Iris who are growing up in a world of multiple challenges. It is my hope that the suggestions it offers will encourage them to find their own vocations and to follow the pilgrim paths along which the Lord is calling them as servants and prophets to others.

---

4 Bruce Duncan, *Social Justice: Fuller Life in a Fairer World*, Mulgrave: Garratt Publishing, 2012.

Introduction

Letter 1

Dear Grandchildren

This book is being written by a recent octogenarian with his six grandchildren in mind. It is not intended to be an academic study but a series of everyday reflections not only on the world you are living in now but also the world you will face throughout the rest of your lives later this century. It also offers suggestions which it is hoped might help you on your journeys through the rest of your lives. It is written from the standpoint of a Catholic layman but also a retired sociology teacher. While I will hopefully draw wisely on my sociological background I will aim to reflect largely on contemporary issues which arise in the course of the writing this book from early 2013. I had no idea how long it would take me to complete it or whether any publisher would risk publishing it. In the end I have had to self-publish since it was not regarded as a commercial proposition! It is written all the time with your generation constantly in mind. My six grandchildren currently range from four to twenty-one years old. So I hope that in time they will read it and find it interesting and hopefully challenging. It would be nice if they would regard it as a series of letters to them, intended to be read when they reach adulthood. It is meant to be thought-provoking and helpful.

Let me begin with a few words about the Catholic dimension. It is now half a century since the Second Vatican Council (1962-65), the most important event in the life of the Roman Catholic Church in the twentieth century. In those days Catholics were expected to be 'docile, deferential, respectful and submissive'. For those who were young adults in the early 1960s, as I was, the Council was a marvellous breath of fresh air, an explosion of excitement and possibilities, an opening up of the Church to dialogue with the world, and an affirmation of the status of lay people as the 'People of God' sharing in Jesus' priesthood, prophetic witness and participation in decision-making. Those who had high hopes of the reforms have often felt frustrated that many of its promises remain unfulfilled but are hopeful that the papacy of Pope Francis will lead to desirable reforms. We are aware that as far as my grandchildren's generation is concerned the Council seems like ancient history; it is not where they are at. I believe this is seriously to underestimate its importance and I will try to discuss this with you later, especially in Part III.

A few days before I started writing the House of Commons had voted in favour of gay marriage. My own view was that this was an unnecessary misuse of a concept and that just as apples and pears though they were both fruit were different, so marriage and civil partnerships were both social relationships, but different. Discussing this at Sunday lunch with one of my sons and his wife it was clear that they did not agree and considered we were betraying our supposed concern for the equality of all people. It was claimed that a high proportion of people in the media industry were 'gay' and that they hadn't chosen that but that it had been God-given. It struck me that there are hints here of generational shifts of understanding and belief and that it was my job to try and reconcile long-standing Christian beliefs with recent scientific discoveries. Dialogue between the Church and the world had been agreed by the Second Vatican Council, and that is a position I hold.

Another 'sign of the times' appeared in the weekend's parish Newsletter. A priest was quoted as saying:

> The Age of Casual Catholicism is over;
>
> The Age of Heroic Catholicism has begun.

He went on to say:

> We can no longer be Catholic by Accident
>
> But instead we need to be Catholic by Conviction.

Wow! What a challenge to servanthood and prophecy. I'd like to take that up in Part IV of this book. But there were also 'signs of the times' in my Monday morning emails from sociologists of religion. For example, an international conference was advertised with the intriguing title:

> Being... Pious in the Age of Facebook, Youtube and Twitter.

You will realise that I am not 'with it' if I confess that I have a suspicion of social media and have never yet gone into Facebook, Youtube or Twitter. But I am aware of such generational differences and in this book hope to dialogue with you about them.

In the spirit of reflecting on issues of the day, I am writing this on the day after Pope Benedict XVI resignation was announced. Even a secularist paper like the *Guardian* recognised that this had not happened for several centuries. It devoted five or more pages to the unexpected announcement and its main editorial offered a reasonably balanced review of the implications. So why is this so significant? It points to the continuing importance of the Catholic Church with 1.2 billion adherents in our modern world and, at least indirectly, to the main theme of this book: what should we be doing to make it a better place.

As far as my sociological background is concerned, I hope it will prove most helpful in trying to understand what it is that is going on in our world today, not only in our own society but also globally. You will all have heard about globalisation, climate change and issues of interdependence both in our own society and indeed globally. These will be the main areas of concern in Parts I and II of this book.

So, what am I proposing to do in this book and these letters? What are my aims in writing to you? I think my main aim is to draw out what it means to be a lay follower of Jesus at this present time, in the first quarter of the twenty-first century. As Catholics we believe that Jesus came down on earth 2000 years ago, lived among us 'in all things except sin', taught us that our primary task is to do the will of God in all things, and that he died to save us from our sins, and rose from the dead to open up for us eternal life with God. What does that mean for your generation where it seems institutional religion is often discounted? In dialoguing with you and your generation, I hope to explore what it means to be a committed lay Catholic in an often hostile and secular world today.

Shortly after the First World War a Belgium priest proposed a three-fold process: *see* (what the issues are), *judge* them (in the light of the Gospel teaching) and then *act* (to challenge whatever was not right). Over the years this has been slightly elaborated into the four-fold pastoral strategy:

- what is the *social reality*?;
- what *social analysis* can we draw on to explain that social reality?;
- what *theological (and scriptural) analysis* helps us to judge the social reality?; and
- what *social action* is appropriate to respond to the social reality in the light of both social and theological analyses?

I propose to follow this sequence in this present book of nine letters. Thus Part I attempts to offer a sketch of the social realities of the world as it is emerging in the second decade of the twenty-first century. Letter 2 will outline some of the global realities and challenges. It will point to the dominance of de-regulated liberal market capitalism and its spread throughout the world and its implications for inequality and the development of developing nations. It will consider the challenges of climate change, population growth, and shortages of water and food. Letter 3 will consider the implications for our own domestic society. We will seek the 'signs of the times' in your everyday lives, the uncertainties you will face in getting an appropriate education, job insecurities, the challenges of family life and of coping with competing demands such as making appropriate provision for increasing life expectancies and the need for care of the elderly, and so on.

These are the social realities. Part II offers an outline of a social analysis of these various domestic and international problems and injustices identified in Part I. It will look at the distribution of power and the built-in inequalities which follow. Letter 4 will look at the prevailing economic, cultural and political relationships and particularly the power of major financial and commercial enterprises which is frequently greater than those of nation-states in the globalised world of today. Letter 5 will consider the attempts to control that power through democratic regulation and persuasion both domestically and internationally through mechanisms such as the United Nations and the International Monetary Fund. What are the chances of mobilising compassion and achieving conciliation between warring factions?

In Part III we will address the issue of what does the Christian faith bring to bear on these issues and realities in a scriptural and theological analysis. In particular it will aim to respond to the call of the Second Vatican Council (1962-65) to read 'the signs of the times' and respond to them in dialogue with the modern world. Thus Letter 6 will review the development of Catholic social teaching since Pope Leo XIII's encyclical *Rerum Novarum* (1891), through to the Second Vatican Council and through the papacies of Pope's John XXIII, Paul VI, John-Paul II, Benedict XVI and Francis I. It will propose a pilgrim, listening, servant Church of the 'People of God' on the move. Letter 7 will go further and suggest the need for a prophetic Church, more counter-cultural in an often hostile and secular world, willing to challenge the powerful in the search for social justice.

Part IV will ask the question: so what do we do? What social action responses do we propose in the light of our social and theological analyses of the social realities of the world in which we all live? Two levels of response will be suggested. In Letter 8 the need for reform of the institutional Church will be considered so that it is missionary to the world as it promotes a counter-culture. It will also ask the question of each individual: how should we respond in our daily lives and actions? What are we called to do in our daily vocations, whatever they might be? How might you make a start in responding to the challenges facing you? The final Letter 9 will discuss how you might respond in solidarity with others and points to a range of campaigning groups which might be helpful. It will conclude by asking how *you* are going to respond as pilgrim, servant and prophet? What do you think Jesus is calling *you* to do with your lives?

This is not intended to be an academic study but an on-going conversation. I have not, therefore, provided reference details for my sources of information. As I have written these chapters over several months I have referred to issues which were in the everyday news. I have used information published in the *Guardian* and *Observer* newspapers, and occasionally government statistical sources published by the Office of National Statistics (ONS). I have found Wikipedia particularly helpful but have generally surfed the internet for evidence, for example of recent reports. You can see that I have attempted to embrace modern technologies! I trust that my use of this material has been appropriate to the idea of an on-going conversation.

The issues I have raised and the examples I have quoted were those hitting the headlines as I was writing. True to that sense of relevance it is appropriate to reflect on the witness of Nelson Mandella who died in the week I revised this first letter. His gift of forgiveness was quite remarkable and humbling and one which the whole world recognised. His search for reconciliation between hitherto warring factions is one which we should all do our best to emulate. The need for it is painfully obvious today in Northern Ireland still, and in Syria, Nigeria and the Central African Republic.

Those of you who have bothered to read this so far are likely to have been baptised as Christians. You will have been given a faith in Jesus, the divine Word of God, who became a human being like us in order to save us from sin and death, and who wishes to communicate and relate with you. I hope you find this short book of nine letters helps you to develop this relationship with Jesus, and that you find it informative, helpful and challenging. It is an invitation to set out on a journey as a *pilgrim* follower of Jesus, our Lord and guide, uncertain where it might lead but full of hope in the knowledge that He will be with you, and committed to become a *servant* of others as He called us to be at the last Supper, and courageous enough to be a *prophet* and challenge many of the taken-for-granted practices and assumptions of life in our contemporary world.

Part I

Social Realities

Letter 2

Global Realities And Challenges

The aim of this letter is to outline for you the main features of the world in which you live and in which you are likely to work, raise a family, and hopefully retire in some sort of security. As I shall argue, this world, and as far as can be predicted the world as it is likely to develop over the next few decades, is likely to present you and your generation with some massive challenges. In this letter I will mainly address the global dimension. Letter 3 will look at how things are likely to develop domestically, in our own society. This is not an exercise in futurology; one cannot with precision predict whether there will be nuclear war, or unanticipated earth shattering disasters such as major volcanic eruptions which damage the earth's food supply, or whatever. But we can note the current realities and trends and ask ourselves how we judge them.

1. Globalisation

As I began to write this letter I came across some notes I had made in January 2010 on a BBC2 series on the 'noughties', that is trends that could be discerned in the first decade of the twenty-first century. Three sessions dealt with changes in British society and I will discuss these further in the next letter. A fourth session dealt with 'the onward march of globalisation' which is a key theme of this letter. If you want to know more about globalisation you could find a useful introduction on the internet in Wikipedia.

Broadly speaking, the concept of 'globalisation' refers to the economic, social, cultural, technological and political processes which are contributing to a growing integration of the world and a growing interdependence between nations and peoples. This process has been going on for centuries, ever since nations began trading with each other. It increased during the centuries of colonialism as European countries sought to extend their influence across the world and open up their domestic markets to cheap sources of raw materials. But it grew more rapidly in the 1970s and 80s with the growth of cheap air travel. More recently developments in information and communications technology, computers and mobile phones have further accelerated this trend. This has presented us with a number of challenges as the following cases demonstrate.

As I write this section there is a massive scandal currently making headlines. It has been discovered that many of the meat dishes sold by large retailers as beef are in fact made with horse meat. While it is generally agreed that this doesn't present any sort of health risk, it is clearly misleading, and probably fraudulent to suggest to gullible customers that these dishes are genuinely made of beef. As I write the full details have yet to be exposed but it has been suggested that the process originated with meat in Romania, which was then exported to commercial enterprises in France and manufactured or processed and packaged in Luxembourg, before being exported to countries like the United Kingdom where products are sold in supermarkets, and to restaurants and schools. Countries involved include Germany, Sweden, Belgium, the Netherlands, Switzerland and Ireland, as well as the UK. This demonstrates the complexity of the chain of international commercial interdependence.

A second example relates to the credit crunch and financial crash of 2008. The origins of the crash were traced back to exaggeratedly careless lending by the US banks to 'sub-prime' lenders, that is poorer people who did not have the resources to continue paying their mortgages when economic conditions worsened. The results were that thousands of poor people lost their homes. Because nobody could afford to buy their houses the lending banks were in great trouble and feared to lend even to other banks; hence the credit crunch. Banks stopped lending and so industrial investment came to a halt. But it didn't stop there. Financial whizz kids sold on the banks' debts wrapped up in a whole range of new packages which were then sold all over the world. Soon it became apparent that banks all over the world had dodgy packages which were worthless. In this country some banks were, in effect, nationalised in order to prevent a total collapse of the banking sector. This was the beginning of the global recession which has lasted five years and is expected to last at least another five years. Greece is a prime example of the knock-on effect and is only able to survive by agreeing stringent austerity measures in return for loans which it must pay back with high rates of interest. The standard of living of millions of people has been severely reduced and this gives rise to social unrest and the potential danger of extremist parties taking over. Other countries like Spain have unemployment rates of one quarter, and over half of the under 25s.

Both these example illustrate the nature of globalisation in the contemporary world. Commercial and financial enterprises are increasingly interlinked. This is greatly facilitated by the rapid developments in information and communications technology especially over the last two decades. It means, for example, that billions of pounds can be moved around practically instantaneously in the search for higher profits. The implications of this are enormous. Generally speaking individual states are just not strong enough to resist concerted attacks on the value of their currencies. This happened to the UK in 1992 when George Soros bet against the value of the pound and forced the UK out of the Exchange Rate Mechanism.

A couple of years ago there was a popular uprising against the dictatorial regime of President Mubarak in Egypt. By all accounts the activists in the uprising were able to organise their resistance using mobile phones and various social media resources. Even in China it is becoming increasingly difficult for the ruling Communist Party to prevent the rapidly expanding affluent working and middle classes from knowing what is going on in the rest of the world. With modern media they are exposed to different and sometimes more attractive cultures which they wish to imitate. This includes not only music but also political rights such as are found in democratic societies. In time this is likely to pose a significant political problem for the current rulers.

We are, perhaps, still too close to the recent technological revolution in information technology to grasp how significant it has already been and what changes it is likely to bring in the future. People of my generation often joke that they need to get their grandchildren to help them with their mobile phones, the internet, and the multitude of 'apps' that are available. A review of predictions about future developments recently noted that 'capitalism has gone digital' and that 'in the automated world, information is more important to the economy than manual labour'. The founder of Facebook, Mark Zuckerberg, claimed that 'by giving people the power to share, we're making the world more transparent'. Another commentator thought that digital technology will enable us to lead absorbing and properly rewarded lives, if we are paid for the information we give, and that we are likely to outgrow our addiction to consumerism and technology. Mm! I rather doubt it! But what seems quite clear is that the recent developments in communications technology have forced us to face the reality of our interdependence.

In sum, there is a complex of economic, technological, cultural and political issues to do with the increasing interactions between all the states in the world which are becoming more and more inter-linked and interdependent. These various and complementary processes are what constitutes globalisation. The world is becoming a 'smaller' place; communications can be instantaneous. Grandparents can speak face-to-face with their grandchildren in Australia using Skype! What happens in one part of the network effects all the other parts.

2. International Regulation

One implication of this is that there is a need for some sort of regulation to control the activities of all the major players, whether they are commercial organisations, or banks or nation states. In the aftermath of the Second World War a series of institutions was set up with the aim of preventing war and mediating conflict and regulating international trading arrangements in the common interest. Or at least that was the theory! Thus the United Nations Organisation was set up in 1945 after World War II to replace the League of Nations, to stop wars and to cope with political disputes. It also aimed to facilitate cooperation in international law, international security, economic development, social progress and human rights. Other outcomes included the UN Declaration of Human Rights which was adopted by the UN General Assembly in 1948 and various international institutions such as the UN High Commission for Refugees (UNHCR) which was established in 1950.

The International Monetary Fund (IMF) was created in 1944 at the Bretton Woods Conference and came into existence in 1945 shortly after the end of World War II. It aimed to stabilise currency exchange rates and assist economic reconstruction. The IMF describes itself as 'working to foster global monetary cooperation, secure financial stability, facilitate international trade, promote high employment and sustainable economic growth, and reduce poverty around the world.' It was set up to assist states in short-term financial difficulty and prevent a recurrence of global depressions such as the world experienced in the 1930s.

The World Bank was also set up at the Bretton Woods Conference in 1944. It is an international financial institution which provides loans to encourage and promote the development of newly independent former colonial states. As I draft this the leaders of some of the most powerful nations in the world are discussing how best to tackle the problems of tax avoidance by some of the most powerful commercial organisations in the world. The challenges of international regulation are ever expanding and there is clearly a long way to go.

It has been suggested that we have moved from the analogue years of the twentieth century to the digital years of the twenty-first century. Among current problems, one is the regulation or control of the internet and the proliferating range of mechanisms of global communication. Recently there was a BBC documentary about the Google Book project. It seems that initially major libraries, such as Harvard University and also the Bodleian Library in Oxford were persuaded by Google to allow all their books to be digitalised in order to extend the opportunities of free access to a much wider public. Initially the universities were quite keen. But in time Google started selling these books, becoming in effect a bookseller. An Authors' Guild in the US took legal action claiming that their copyright safeguards had been infringed and there was a $125 million settlement. But at a later stage a US District judge rejected the settlement saying that it gave Google the ability to 'exploit' books without the permission of copyright owners. The French national library bitterly opposed the scheme as did some German authors. The whole affair does point to the conflict between better access for more people but also the dangers of monopoly power. It also points to the global reach of giant internet corporations.

All was not rosy as the focus on the millennium development goals attempted to spotlight. At a meeting of the United Nations in 2000 all 193 member states agreed to the following eight Millennium Development Goals to be achieved by 2015:

1. Eradicating extreme poverty and hunger, and halving the proportion of people living on less than $1 a day;
2. Achieving universal primary education for both girls and boys;
3. Promoting gender equality and empowering women, and in particular eliminating gender disparity at all levels of education;
4. Reducing mortality rates of the under fives by two-thirds;
5. Improving maternal health, reducing the maternal mortality rate by three-quarters;
6. Combating HIV/AIDS, malaria, and other diseases; in particular begin to reverse the spread of HIV/AIDS and the incidence of malaria and other diseases;
7. Ensuring environmental sustainability, and reversing the loss of environmental resources; and
8. Developing a global partnership for development, in particular an open, rule-based, predictable, non-discriminatory trading and financial system, paying particular attention to the special needs of the least developed nations; ensuring debt levels are sustainable in the long term; making available essential drugs and the benefits of information and communications technologies in developing countries.

These targets give some idea of the scope of problems and challenges at the global level. At a UN review summit in 2010 some progress was reported in most areas but there were concerns that insufficient attention was being paid to women's empowerment and vulnerability to poverty and its consequences. Accordingly major new commitments to women's and children's health and initiatives in the struggle against poverty, hunger and disease were announced.

3. Recent Developments

In the past half-century there have been some important developments which have had global significance. For example, in 1989 the communist regimes of the Soviet Union and Eastern Europe suddenly collapsed and the end of the 'Cold War' was celebrated. Some interpreted this as the victory of de-regulated liberal capitalism which had experienced great economic developments over several decades. It seemed that this economic system had self-evidently defeated totalitarian state control of the economy. Even the communist leaders of China began to develop a market form of capitalism. These developments seemed to offer the opportunity for endless economic growth for all the peoples of the world.

The economic growth of countries like China, India and Brazil has been extremely rapid. Since China initiated market reforms in 1978 its average annual growth rates have been around 10% a year and over 600 million people, about half its population, have been lifted out of poverty. It recently became the world's second largest economy and current projections suggest that by 2040 China's share of global GDP (Gross Domestic Product) will be 40% compared with that of 14% for the US and only 5% for the European Union. These are potentially momentous changes which will undoubtedly influence your lives.

For the first three decades after independence India's economy was largely inspired by socialist principles and growth rates were only around 1% a year. Since the mid-1980s there has been a gradual economic liberalisation and in the late 2000s growth rates reached over 7%, mainly in services such as those outsourced from Britain. Major problems include a labour force growing more rapidly than employment and hence increasing levels of unemployment, and high levels of corruption. It is currently the world's fourth largest economy and predicted to rise to third by 2020. Brazil is currently the world's ninth largest economy and is predicted to become the seventh by 2020 and fifth at a later stage. In recent years its annual growth rate has averaged 5%.

The economic and political implications of these changes in the years ahead are likely to be enormous. Within your lifetimes China, India and Brazil are likely to have economies which dwarf that of the United States which has been in the driving seat for the past seven decades since the Second World War. There are sure to be tensions as such huge shifts of economic power from the US and the European Union to the more recently developing nations are played out. In time these shifts of economic power will require changes in the composition and decision-making processes of the major international financial institutions such as the International Monetary Fund and the World Bank. The US will no longer have de facto veto power. It is not obvious that either the US or the European Union have even begun to adjust to these likely developments.

Of course there are close links between economic and political and military power. Since the collapse of Communism in 1989 the US has basked in being the world's only superpower and has demonstrated its strength in its response to the attack on the World Trade Centre in 2001 with wars in Iraq and Afghanistan. Both those wars were highly controversial, resulted in huge losses of life, and had outcomes which remain uncertain. But what is clearly on the table is a shift of political power as the newly emerging economic powers flex their muscles and demand a much bigger say in the management of conflicts on the global stage. For example, the five permanent members of the UN Security Council, China, France, Russia, the UK and USA, represented the great powers considered to be the victors of the Second World War nearly seven decades ago. These no longer reflect the de facto power differentials in the twenty-first century.

4. Inequality

Another major problem is that of increasing inequality both within and between nations. The US and UK are among the most unequal nations in the world. In the 1980s in both countries the income gap between the rich and the poor jumped dramatically and has substantially remained very high. Some would see high levels of inequality as 'structural violence'. A recent book entitled *The Spirit Level*, used comparative statistics both to compare nations with different levels of inequality, and different income groups within nations. They provided a great deal of evidence to show that higher levels of inequality were associated with higher levels of a great range of general health and social problems. These included levels of infant mortality, teenage pregnancies, murder, imprisonment, mental illness, use of drugs, obesity, children's experiences of conflict; and lower levels of life expectancy, maths and literacy scores, aspirations, social mobility, trust, women's status and general wellbeing. There is always the danger, too, that the perception of unjust inequalities may lead to social unrest and a collapse of social cohesion. There were clear signs of this potential in the urban riots in the UK in 2011 and on the streets of Athens and Madrid as austerity measures began to bite.

In my view inequality is one of the greatest challenges facing Christians today. It seems to be associated with the dominant economic ideology of liberal capitalism which favours those with economic power and labels those without as 'shirkers' or 'skivers'. The freedom of the market is paramount and it is regarded as entirely up to the individual to cope and his or her fault if they don't 'make it'. At its worst, as for example in the US Tea Party, there is a hatred of anything to do with the state. There is little or no conception of shared concerns or of communal interests on behalf of the wider society. Individualism is uncontrolled and there is no sense of the common good such as universal health care, education, care of the elderly, and so on. With this view the financial sector of the economy rules supreme. High levels of profit in the short term is the only criterion of success for commercial enterprises and inevitably longer term needs, such as responding to the challenges of climate change or of an ageing population, are neglected. At the very least, high levels of inequality are unfair and unjust and a major challenge to the Christian conscience.

5. Resource Shortages

(a) Oil

One significant aspect of the processes of globalisation is the evidence of increasing competition for major resources such as oil and gas. Oil is the massive driver of the global economy and historically the developed nations have imported the bulk of their needs, for example from the Middle East. Britain had a long and murky past with Persia or today's Iran and Iraq, massive exporters of oil. In 1968 the Organisation of Arab Petroleum Exporting Countries (OAPEC) tried to put pressure on western support for Israel. They increased the price of oil and reduced production. This led to a global oil shortage and oil prices quadrupled. In the UK the Cabinet announced a three-day week in certain industries and inflation rose to over 27% in 1975.There was a great deal of social unrest.

In recent years both the US and UK have struggled to maintain good relations with the countries of the Middle East. They have turned a blind eye to human rights concerns because of their need for oil. Both countries reacted militarily when Iraq invaded Kuwait in 1991 and both countries seek close relations with Saudi Arabia which is the world's largest oil producer. More than one quarter of the global production of crude oil comes from Saudi Arabia, Iran, Iraq, the United

Arab Emirates and Kuwait. Estimates vary widely as to whether or not there is likely to be a serious shortage of oil within the next decade or so. There is an ongoing debate between those who believe oil production will soon peak and oil companies who are optimistic that new technologies will extend the life of oil beyond present estimates. These suggest that at present rates of consumption oil will last for 40 years. But it is pointed out that by then the world population might have increased by several billion and that more of it will be industrialised and hence oil dependent.

What is certain is that it is a finite resource likely to run out at some point, probably in your life times. With the rapid growth of economies such as that of China, competition for oil is likely to grow and the price of oil rise sharply. This will inevitably lead to growing tensions between nations and even the threat of war in order to secure access to oil. Another major consequence is likely to be serious global warming and climate change which we will discuss later in this letter.

(b) Water

A second major resource, the shortages of which have the potential to lead to tension, conflict and even war, is water. The UN Conference on Trade and Development (UNCTAD) has pointed to concerns about water shortages. The evidence is imposing. It is estimated that 3.4 million people, nearly all of them in the developing world, die each year from a water-related disease, poor hygiene and sanitation. Around one billion people in the developing world do not have access to clean, safe drinking water. As demand for scarce supplies of water increase so will the cost and the dangers to political and social stability. The UN Food and Agriculture Organisation (FAO) has estimated that by 2025 1.9 billion people will be living in countries or regions with absolute water scarcity, and two-thirds of the world population could be under stress conditions of limited water access. A water crisis is defined as a situation where the available unpolluted water in a region is less than the demand. There are several principal manifestations of such a crisis:

1. Inadequate access to safe drinking water for about 884 million people (or one in eight of the world's population);
2. Inadequate access to water for sanitation and waste disposal for 2.5 billion people (or one-third of the world's population); this kills around 4,000 children every day, more than HIV/AIDS, malaria and TB combined;
3. Excessive use of groundwater leading to diminishing agricultural yields;
4. Overuse and pollution of water resources harming biodiversity; and
5. Regional conflicts over scarce water resources sometimes leading to warfare.

The charity Water Aid points out that without basic water and sanitation services people will be trapped in a cycle of poor health, limited education and little opportunity to work themselves out of it. According to the UN, with rapid population growth and increased industrial demand water consumption has tripled over the past fifty years. Thus the OECD had predicted that by 2030 nearly half of the world's population will be living in areas of high 'water stress' and strategists from Israel to Central Asia are said to be preparing for strife. Last year the Energy Secretary warned that water wars were a real prospect as states struggled with the effects of climate change, growing demand for water and declining resources. More than 30 countries have been involved in 'water wars' and 145 countries share lakes and river basins the use of which is governed by cooperative agreements. But in Africa, where a quarter of the population already lives with chronic water stress, water is increasingly seen as a source of potential conflict between nations eager to secure their future harvests.

(c) Food

Turning now to food production and shortages. Farming accounts for 70% of the world's use of fresh water that is globally extracted for human use. The UN predicts that irrigation demands will grow by 50-100% by 2025. The world is said to be facing a serious problem of food security. The challenge is to produce enough safe and nutritious food in a sustainable way for a growing world population estimated to reach 9 billion by 2050, well within your lifetimes. Shortages lead inevitably to price rises beyond the pockets of poor people, and hence possible starvation. There is a real danger of increasing stress levels having serious social and political implications. Large price rises of 70-130% of staple foods in 2008 caused riots or civil unrest in 36 countries, especially in African and Asia. The world needs to grow more food and the World Bank estimates cereal production needs to grow by 50% and meat production by 85% to meet demand in 2030. But water stress and desertification is reducing the amount of arable land and many pests are becoming resistant to insecticides. It is estimated that around one quarter of crops can be lost to pests and diseases. Huge quantities of food are lost as a result of underdeveloped infrastructure and transport. In the US just over a quarter of the food available for consumption was lost in retailing. In the UK it has been estimated that 4.4 million apples, 5.1 million potatoes, 2.8 million tomatoes and 1.6 million bananas are binned every day.

In sum, we have indicated that there are serious dangers of global oil, water and food shortages with the potential to lead to serious conflicts and even wars between nations. Furthermore, because of global population increases and the rapid industrialisation of large countries like China, India and Brazil, such tensions are likely to grow over the next few decades. This demonstrates again the growing interdependence of the nations of the world and the urgent need for international cooperation and systems of conflict resolution between nations.

6. New Forms of Conflict

In the contemporary period of globalisation there are other forms of conflict apart from inter-state conflict.

(a) Genocide

For example, the international community has had to learn how to cope with genocide within a nation. It failed to prevent the appalling genocide in Rwanda and only belatedly intervened to prevent a second round of genocide in Kosovo. In the past couple of years there have been great uncertainties about the appropriate way to respond to the civil war in Syria. It seems that international law, as presently formulated, inhibits intervention in the internal affairs of any nation state. A report by the International Commission on Intervention and State Sovereignty aimed to promote a comprehensive global debate on the issue and reconcile the international community's responsibility to act in the face of massive violations of humanitarian norms, such as the use of gas, while respecting the rights of sovereign states. Implicit in this is the recognition that we are all members of a global community in which at least a basic minimum of rights ought to be respected.

(b) Terrorism

Recent atrocities in New York, Washington, Madrid, London, Nairobi and elsewhere have drawn attention to an ugly side of globalising processes. People and nations now realise that small numbers of committed terrorists with a perceived grievance and an ideology which justifies violence, for example against 'westernisation', could threaten not only large numbers of people anywhere in the world but also the stability of the global economy itself, and with it the livelihoods of billions of people. With hindsight it could be argued that it was a major error to initiate a 'war on terror' against Al-Qaeda rather than seek international collaboration in the search for small groups of criminals. The perception of criminal violence as a global threat to all might have generated a remarkable coalition of previously hostile or suspicious nations in seeking an appropriate response. It would also emphasise the interdependence of all people on earth. One suggestion was that the 'new wars' of non-state terrorism aimed to mobilise people on the basis of their identities. Religious differences have clearly been significant in some recent and contemporary conflicts. Terrorism aims to destabilise and foment hatred and fear. An appropriate response seems to be a strategy of winning hearts and minds by promoting cosmopolitan civic values favouring openness, toleration and participation.

(c) Cyber Attacks

You are living in a new world which requires new international arrangements in order to cope with novel challenges. One such challenge is cyber attack on a society's critical infrastructure: telecommunications, energy, banking and finance, transportation and government services. This is not just a national security matter but increasingly an international security problem requiring the building of consensus-creating coalitions, transnational surveillance and cooperation, and the sharing of information in this new age of uncertainty. Recent revelations about the extent of surveillance conducted by the British GCHQ and US NSA have drawn attention to the difficult balance between the individual's right to personal privacy and the state's duty to ensure security for its citizens. There is little doubt that this will be an increasingly important issue in your own lifetimes.

7. Global Warming

2012 was an extraordinary year as far as the weather in the UK was concerned. The early months of the year saw a severe drought, the serious depletion of water reserves in our reservoirs and threats of hose pipe bans. But by the end of the year we had had to cope with the wettest year on record and many areas of the country had experienced very severe flooding. The jet stream which has a large influence on our weather patterns had shifted significantly and was thought to have had a major influence on the topsy-turvy nature of our experiences in 2012. Inevitably, queries were raised about the impact of global warming on climate change and that what we were experiencing was only one part of a major phenomenon which was global in scope.

Since the early years of the twentieth century the earth's mean surface temperature has increased by around 0.8°C and various models produced by the Intergovernmental Panel on Climate Change (IPCC) predict that it will increase by a further 1-6°C during your lifetimes in the twenty-first century. A major cause of global warming has been the steady increase in the level of greenhouse gases in the atmosphere as a consequence of processes of industrialisation since the nineteenth century. The absorption and emission of infrared radiation by gases in the atmosphere has resulted in the warming of the earth's lower atmosphere and surface. Human activity since the onset of industrialisation in the nineteenth century has resulted in increases in carbon dioxide in the atmosphere of over one-third and of methane by one and a half times since 1750. These levels are higher than at any time in the past 800,000 years. Fossil fuel burning has produced about three-quarters of the carbon dioxide increase over the past 20 years with most of the rest has resulting from deforestation.

The anticipated effects of an increase in global temperatures include a rise in sea levels, a change in the amount and pattern of rainfall, as well as a probable expansion of subtropical deserts. The effects are expected to be largest in the Arctic regions and we are already familiar with images of polar bears isolated on small islands of melting ice and of evidence of the serious melting of glaciers in recent decades. More extreme weather patterns are predicted including heat waves, droughts and water rationing, heavy rainfall and flooding. In the past year or two such extremes have been experienced even in the UK. In low-lying countries like Bangladesh the consequences of serious rises in sea levels would be catastrophic. Other predictions include serious threats to food security from decreasing crop yields and loss of habitat.

Mitigation of the anticipated consequences by a reduction of greenhouse gases is the main international policy response. Most countries are parties to the United Nations Framework Convention on Climate Change (UNFCCC) and have adopted a range of policies designed to reduce greenhouse gas emissions and assist adaptation to global warming. There is formal agreement that future global warming should be limited to 2°C above the pre-industrial age level. However, reports by international agencies in 2011 warned that efforts introduced so far may be inadequate to meet the UNFCCC 2°C target.

Recent figures show that China produces nearly one quarter of the world's carbon dioxide while the US produces about one-sixth. But the US emissions/person is 17.6 tons of carbon dioxide per year compared to China's 6.2 tons. The UK figure is 7.9 tons carbon dioxide/person per year compared to India's 1.7 and Brazil's 2.2 tons carbon dioxide/person per year. Clearly, reducing carbon dioxide emissions is a highly political issue since western societies have gone through a period of rapid industrialisation and have been responsible for most of the increases. Inevitably, newly industrialising countries like China, India and Brazil, with their huge populations, are not keen to have their processes of development inhibited by the demands of the developed nations. But in a globalised world where no one is exempt from real global problems such as global warming, there is a need for serious international collaborative efforts in the interests of all the peoples of the earth. This will be a serious challenge to your generation.

8. Migration

Recently I watched a documentary on BBC about 'Good Italy, Bad Italy' just before the result of the Italian election was announced. One of the startling pieces of information which shook me was that a million young people, mainly graduates, had emigrated from Italy in search of better opportunities to use their skills than they anticipated at home. Recent census results in the UK indicated that over one half of the population of London had been born abroad. London is one of the most cosmopolitan cities in the world, the home of many people from all over the world. This is happening more and more in our globalised world and is, in fact, an important characteristic of globalisation.

The International Organisation for Migration estimates the number of international migrants has increased in recent years to around 214 million or 3.1% of the world's population. Just under one half of these are women. Estimated remittances sent by migrants to their country of origin have also increases rapidly to an estimated $440 billion in 2010. Of this some $325 billion was sent by migrants to developing countries such as India and for many countries was a large percentage of their GNP. A BBC report indicated that roughly one third of migrants had migrated to Europe. This is perhaps not surprising and reflects relations between former colonial territories. In the US some 22 million workers, 16% of the labour force, are foreign born. In Australia and New Zealand around one quarter of the labour force is foreign born. In the UK in 2002, according to the OECD, there were about 1½ million workers or 5% of the labour force who were foreign born. The UN High Commissioner for Refugees reports that in 2010 there were around 15.4 million refugees. By far the biggest group of refugees at the beginning of the decade, around 2½ million, were from Afghanistan.

In modern times transnational migration has been encouraged by industrialisation and reached a peak of 3 million a year from European countries, mainly to the US, in the early years of the twentieth century. The two world wars, the ending of the colonial period for European states in the post-war period, the partition of Pakistan-India, various ethnic conflicts, and the global movement from subsistence agriculture to urban areas, have all contributed to massive migrations. Migration in search of work became a popular way for impoverished people in developing countries to obtain sufficient income to survive. The recent tragedy and loss of life of would-be immigrants at the island of Lampedusa have drawn attention to the terrible dangers such migrants face. At the same time industry in the developed countries coped with labour shortages by encouraging inward migration. We are perhaps most aware of migrant workers in our own country when we notice the large numbers of ethnic medical staff in hospitals or in care homes. We need to recognise that this represents a form of 'brain drain' from poor countries to rich ones. In sum, labour migration is an important characteristic of the processes of globalisation in the contemporary world. Apart from its economic advantages, there are also potential problems of social and ethnic conflicts, such as anger by indigenous workers that their pay is being squeezed as a result of a supply of workers willing to work for lower wages or under poorer conditions.

9. Global Interdependence

In this letter I have endeavoured to convey a sense that there is a wide range of forces in the world in which we live which together are making us face the reality that we are 'all in this world together', that we largely share the same expectations about life for economic and political well-being, that we depend on each other, and that we are all interdependent. In the digital twenty-first century the barriers to knowledge about other people's lives are being dissolved. Expectations are being harmonised. This is leading to a dramatic acceleration in the transformations of the economies and political systems of developing societies. Suddenly China has revolutionised its economy, at least partially along liberal capitalist lines, and is on the point of becoming the largest economy in the world. As its recently emergent middle classes become more aware of political freedoms in the so-called developed societies through ready access to mass media portrayals of alternative possibilities and as a result of international tourism, they are likely to call for political changes.

These emergent pressures for 'more' of everything are certain to lead to increasing competition for, and consequently higher prices for, vital resources which are in short supply. We are currently experiencing this in the case of energy prices. There are other effects, for example of food speculation, which might severely damage the lives of poor farmers. Shortages of vital resources are also likely to lead to tensions and even wars. The logic of interdependence is that some internationally agreed mechanism for resolving disputes and arbitrating between competing claims is necessary. One can see signs of these developments, for example in the painfully slow progress being made to cope with the dangers of global warming, a problem which is clearly going to affect everyone.

In this letter we have reviewed the economic, political, cultural and technological evidence for a growing interdependence among the nations of the world. These are clearly challenging trends and the future is not at all clear. In your lifetime there are likely to be major conflicts over scarce resources such as oil, water and food. New forms of non-state conflict such as ethnic genocides and terrorism have been noted. Migration, not only of refugees in search of safety and liberty but also of those searching for regular employment, create further tensions. Two conclusions seem to stand out. Firstly, you live in a finite earth with a steadily increasing population with its growing demand for food. Problems such as global warming affect everyone and demonstrate that we are all interdependent. Secondly, solutions to such problems require international collaboration and regulation. In my next letter we will look at the challenges which are to be found in our own society.

Letter 3

Domestic Realities

In the previous letter I briefly reviewed some of the challenges your generation is likely to face as a result of economic, social, political, technological and cultural developments which together make up the process of globalisation which is resulting in a growing recognition of our interdependence in an increasingly interconnected world. In this letter I will review some of the domestic realities which you will inevitably have to face up to. Chief among these are likely to be the changing nature of employment and increasing international competition, the impact of new technology, the widening of the gap between the rich few and the many poor and the social and political consequences of increasing inequality, the problems of access to housing, the responses to increasing life expectancy and the demands on resources of an increasing population of elderly people in care, and so on. In sum, as far as one can predict, things are not going to be easy for your generation. It is one purpose of this book to raise your awareness of these realities and in later letters to offer a map to negotiate your journey through your lives based on the principle of following Jesus as best one can.

1. Economic Realities: Debt, Deficit and Consumerism

The President of the European Parliament has complained that Europe has spent around 700 billion euros rescuing its banks but may have lost an entire generation of young people in the process. Some 26 million people are unemployed across the EU including one in every two young people in Greece, Spain and parts of Italy and Portugal. In this country the situation is not quite so bad but even so, nearly one million young people aged 16-24 (or 21%) are unemployed and there are no obvious signs that things are going to improve in the short-term.

As I started writing on a Monday morning I skimmed Saturday's paper. It gave a useful outline of the sorts of economic realities we are facing at the current time. First of all there is a pervading sense of injustice that the major banks which were largely instrumental in creating the economic crisis we are currently experiencing are still paying what seemed to the Trades Union Congress (TUC) General Secretary like 'obscene' bonuses to large numbers of top bankers while many thousands of poor people are having their benefits cut and voluntary food banks are providing food for increasing numbers of people. Barclays, which had earlier in the year been fined £390 million for rigging the Libor benchmark interest rate, paid 428 of its employees over £1 million in 2012 and 55 of these earned £2.5 million, while over 71,000 of its employees were paid £25,000 or less. At the other end of the scale it is anticipated that the so-called 'bedroom tax', designed to force tenants out of under-occupied social housing will generate hunger and risk the eviction of some benefits claimants.

In the UK wealth distribution is highly skewed towards the top 1%.The richest 1% own very nearly one quarter of marketable wealth while the poorer 50% owned only 6%. A report entitled 'An Anatomy of Economic Inequality in the UK' in 2010 showed that the household wealth of the top

10% of the population stood at £853,000, one hundred times higher than the average wealth of the poorest 10% which was around £8,800, a sum which included cars and other possessions. In sum, you are growing up in a very unequal society. It is evidence such as this that is prompting talk about mansion taxes and also firmer action against tax avoidance.

Five years have passed since the start of the current financial crisis and global recession. In the UK the situation is reminiscent of the great depression in the years before the Second World War. Almost every year the Government spends more than it raises in taxes, thus increasing the national debt and resultant interest charges. Our annual budget deficit reached £171 billion in 2009/10, which works out at an annual overspend of £2,800 for every person in the UK each year. At the end of 2012 the national debt was £1,111 billion or nearly 71% of our annual Gross Domestic Product (GDP). This works out at £18,220 for every man, woman and child in the UK. Like many other nations we were living beyond our means and the political response was to usher in 'an age of austerity'. The independent Office for Budget Responsibility has pointed out that austerity has knocked nearly 1.4% off GDP in the past two years. Nationally we tried to tighten our belts and reduce our annual deficit, largely by introducing massive cutbacks in our public services. Inevitably it was the poor, the most vulnerable and women who suffered most and this creates a serious challenge of fairness and equity. It is women, who make up nearly two-thirds of public sector employment and over three-quarters of the workforce of the National Health Service (NHS) and local government who are most vulnerable to the cuts of one million public sector jobs over the next five years. This is the situation as I write this letter. In recent months the effects have been only too obvious on the High Street as major retailers such as HMV, Jessops, and Comet have been forced into administration.

A BBC documentary in 2010 referred to what it called 'property porn' and suggested it was the post-war 'baby boomers' who profited from the property bubble (up to the financial crisis of 2007/8). They claimed there was evidence for a SKI culture ('spend the kids' inheritance') among the 'grandboomers' who were now spending the proceeds of the property boom in a 'flight from maturity'. This was at the expense of the younger generation who would have no jobs, no property, and no pensions. Unlike the older generation, their grandchildren today, that is your generation, would have to pay to go to university, leave with debt, find it difficult to get a job and get into the housing market, and would have no pensions. Pensioners now outnumber the under 16s so there is potential for conflict between the generations. At the very least they will be in competition for scarce resources and benefits.

What has happened in recent decades has been the loss of inhibitions about debt. Whereas my generation was brought up in the early post-war years on an ethic of saving for future purchases, known as the ethic of 'deferred gratification', the emergence of hire purchase, credit cards, and relatively cheap loans, generated a culture shift of major proportions. People lost their inhibitions about debt; self-indulgence and the instant gratification of desires led to 'consumerism', an obsession with consumer spending and keeping up with current fashions, and a fundamentally different economy. After the credit crunch and financial crisis of 2008, there was a sudden awareness that banks, multinationals, and nations were all caught up in a major crisis over their debt levels, as I mentioned above. Whereas two generations ago it was taken for granted that you would only get a mortgage after saving a sizeable deposit and that at marriage you would have very little in the way of furniture which would have to be saved for over many months, many young couples today postpone marriage until they have purchased all the status gadgets considered necessary (cars, kitchen equipment, the latest TVs, and so on).

In some respects the policy responses to the problems of deficit and debt have seemed confused and contradictory as attempts have been made both to reduce debt by making substantial cuts in public services but also to stimulate growth. As I write this in 2013 the future for your generation in particular looks bleak for possibly another five to ten years. It seems that spending patterns you might have grown up with and regarded as natural will need to be severely curtailed and this might be quite a reality shock for you. It is not surprising that the President of the European Parliament warned that with 26 million people unemployed across the EU, including one in every two young people in Greece, Spain and parts of Italy and Portugal, that we might have 'lost' an entire generation in the process.

2. Employment and New Technology

There have been some dramatic shifts in employment patterns over recent decades. For example, there were around 1.5 million people employed as domestic servants in 1901. The popular TV series 'Downton Abbey' indicated that domestic service was beginning to change in the 1920s. A recent Labour Force Survey showed that while only around 65,000 people are currently employed as domestic workers in the UK, on the other hand over 6 million people employ occasional domestic help, such as cleaners, up one million over the past decade.

A second example is the number of miners. In 1900 1,100,000 miners were employed in the UK. By 1950 the number employed by the National Coal Board (NCB) was around 700,000 and this had fallen to 634,000 in 1960. Following the collapse of the Miners' Strike in 1984/5 and the regular closure of inefficient pits, the number now has fallen to only 5,000.

A third example is agricultural labour. Over half a century of farm mechanisation has resulted in a steady decline in the numbers employed on farms to 526,000 or 1.7% of the total labour force in 2009. But the seasonal nature of the work is indicated by the fact that in recent times the proportion of part-time workers has increased from 21% in 1984 to 43% twenty years later.

A fourth example is manufacturing which started to decline in the 1960s and by 2010 accounted for only 8% of the workforce, though it generated 12% of the country's national output. In areas where there have been major structural shifts in employment, unemployment rates remain high, especially among the low skilled male manual workers.

Unlike agriculture and manufacturing, employment in the services sector has gone steadily upwards. It is currently the dominant sector in the UK economy and contributes over three-quarters of GDP. It includes the creative industries, education, health and social work (including the NHS), financial and business services, hotels, restaurants, other social and personal services, real estate and renting activities, tourism, transport, storage and communications, and wholesale and retail trade. There are 5.7 million people working in the public sector but this is likely to fall as a result of proposed budget cuts.

Another noticeable trend is the steady increase in the proportion of women working from 53% in 1971 to 66% in 2011 while the corresponding figures for men have declined from a peak of 92% in 1971 to 76% in 2011. Many only have part-time work but generally benefit from flexible working hours. They are to be found in particular in the service sector and in the public sector where they are particularly vulnerable to proposed cuts. Working women have typically delayed having children and, it seems, were particularly badly hit by the collapse of the housing market around 2008.

One problem many families are facing is the cost of child care. If women are to be enabled to return to paid work after child-bearing, the costs of childcare must not exceed their income from employment. Yet childcare costs are reported to be rising at twice the rate of inflation and in London can reach £14,000 a year for a full-time place. The Daycare Trust reports that for many parents childcare costs can be higher than their rent or mortgage payments.

The number of self-employed has risen by over one-third of a million in the past four years. Over three million people in work want longer hours; such underemployment has increased by over one million since 2008. Recent Labour Market Surveys have pointed to the increase of flexibility in employment such as the exploitative use of 'zero hour contracts'. Such developments, all of which point to the increasing insecurity of employment, are attributed to the pressures of international competition resulting from the processes of globalisation, and Government policies to achieve more flexible labour markets by curtailing the rights of workers.

A worrying aspect of Britain's economic prospects is that we currently have a high and persistent trade deficit, in spite of an effective devaluation of around 30% in the value of the pound sterling since 2007 which should have made it easier to sell our goods abroad. This is attributed to an increase in the demand for consumer goods and a decline in manufacturing and oil and gas production. Annual growth rates have been systematically lower than those of major competitors. All this relates to the impact of globalisation which we discussed in the previous letter. It seems we have lost the productive capacity to respond; this is a major structural matter with long-term consequences for your future employment and standard of living. It seems that there are serious issues which require long-term policies, not simply short-term ones of achieving economic growth and avoiding recession.

These are all trends and problems which you will have to face over the next few decades as you complete your education, seek employment and probably start a family. It would be a good idea to be realistic about your prospects as well as reflect on an appropriate Christian response to them in the light of the suggestions I will offer in Letters 6 and 7.

People of my generation are probably not in the best position to suggest what influence new technologies might have in your lives, for example in employment. But for what it is worth, the following are some suggestions which I hope might be helpful.

One consequence of the emergence of the digital age with new and readily accessible IT gadgets and attendant lifestyles has been the reinvention of a hidden youth culture with its text messaging and wide use of Facebook, Twitter, YouTube and other social media behind closed doors. The power of these new devices was dramatically brought home to the world a couple of years ago during the popular protests in the Middle East referred to as the 'Arab Spring'. It is perhaps too soon to be sure of the long-term social, political and cultural implications of developments in information and communications technologies. One favourable assessment is that the new technologies fundamentally change labour relations and the work process, encouraging more flexible arrangements and the individualisation of work. On the other hand, since I first drafted this paragraph there have been dramatic revelations about the comprehensive nature of surveillance by the security services in the UK and USA. These suggest the need to be vigilant against any trends to reduce individual freedom in the interests of a 'Big Brother' state or of large commercial organisations. So, be on your guard!

3. Poverty and Increasing Inequality

In this section I will explore the realities of social inequality in Britain today. We are one of the richest half dozen societies in the world yet there is a great deal of poverty and levels of inequality have risen sharply since the 1980s. There is strong evidence that extreme forms of inequality are harmful to a whole range of public health issues and well-being. A great deal of polemical venom has been directed at so-called work 'skivers' and benefits' 'scroungers' but the evidence suggests that this is almost totally misconceived. Nationally, Labour Market Statistics suggest that there are around 450,000 job vacancies but with two and a half million unemployed, this means five or six applicants for every job. The situation is very much worse in areas of high unemployment. You might recall the riots of a couple of years ago. One of the grievances then was the very high level of unemployment. One M.P. pointed out that there were over 30 job seekers for every full-time job vacancy in his constituency.

A recent Poverty and Social Exclusion report of the Joseph Rowntree Foundation estimated that '6.1 million people in working households are now living in poverty – a number that exceeds the 5.1 million people in workless households in poverty.' A recent book arguing that it was time to end the 'myth of the welfare scrounger', pointed out that 'almost 7 million working age adults are living in extreme financial stress, despite being in employment and largely independent of state support. In addition, 2.2 million children live on the edge of, or in, poverty, despite one or both adults earning low to middle income.'

A month or so ago the BBC ran a series of documentaries entitled '*Growing up Poor*', focusing on the problems of teenagers with no family support, no resources, no qualifications, no jobs, no hope, plenty of stigma and so on. We recently went to see the well-reviewed film '*Les Miserables*'. The plight of the poor struggling to escape from the vicious circle of poverty and starvation, theft or prostitution, harsh prison terms, and inability to earn a decent living was strongly emphasised. What struck me when I saw the film was how similar the problems of the poor were today compared to those of two hundred years ago even if the scale of the problems today was not so great and has been ameliorated by Welfare State benefits and safeguards.

Today thousands of people in the UK regularly go hungry because they do not have enough money to make ends meet. They face impossible choices between eating and heating, feeding their children or paying the rent. Among the many reasons are redundancy, illness, benefit delays, domestic violence, debt, family breakdown and paying the additional heating costs in a harsh winter. The Trussell Trust reports that 13 million people in the UK live below the poverty line. A sign of the costs of the present recession and welfare cutbacks is the fact that the number of food banks has almost doubled in the past year and the number of people fed by food banks nationwide rose from 129,000 in 2011-12 to an estimated 290,000 in 2012-13. The tenfold increase in the use of food banks since the start of the recession has led one senior UN official to warn that it could represent a human rights abuse.

As I mentioned in the previous letter, in 2009 two academics published *The Spirit Level* with the intriguing subtitle 'why more equal societies almost always do better'. The main finding from this comparative statistical study was that the more unequal societies, like the US and UK, had lower life expectancies and higher levels of health and social problems. The evidence shows a big jump in the gap between the incomes of the richest and poorest 10 per cent in Britain since the late 1980s. The poorest tenth of the population now have only around 1.3% of the country's total income and the second poorest tenth have 4%. In contrast the richest tenth have 31% and the second richest tenth have 15%. One measure of inequality is the Gini coefficient where with a score of 1.0 there is maximum inequality, and zero where there is equal distribution. The lower the Gini coefficient the more equal the society. The Gini coefficient which measures overall income inequality in the UK is now higher than at any time in the last thirty years. The OECD has reported that income inequality in the UK is growing faster than in any other rich country. The top 10% have annual incomes twelve times greater than the bottom 10%, up from eight times greater in 1985.

This is another area where you need to be aware of what sort of society it is that you will be trying to take part in through education, getting a job and hopefully entering the housing market. In some respects it is rather bleak with high levels of poverty and inequality. Hopefully this will inspire you to take some sort of action to seek a better, fairer and more equitable society. We will follow this up further in Letters 8 and 9.

4. Changing Family Structures and Demographic Change

One of the most dramatic demographic changes which has taken place in my lifetime has been the incredible increase in average life expectancy. Whereas in the 1960s the average life expectancy was 71, today it is 80. On the basis of current trends it is estimated that between 2010 and 2030 the number of people aged over 65 will increase by over one half and the number of people aged over 85 will double. Half of those born after 2007, which means one in two of your children, will live to over 100. At the same time there will be large increases in the proportion of the elderly with severe disabilities or chronic diseases. One estimate is that unless treatment and cures improve, the incidence of the five most chronic conditions among the over-65s - arthritis, heart disease, stroke, diabetes and dementia – will increase by 25% by 2020 and more than 50% by 2030. The Institute of Fiscal

Studies estimates the NHS would have a shortfall of around £30 billion, nearly one-quarter of its annual budget.

Such changes will pose all sorts of challenges to your generation. What sort of long-term care can these elderly people expect and how will it be paid for? Can the welfare state principle of 'universality', i.e. same basic support for all regardless of income or status, continue? What sort of pensions policies are appropriate? Should there be a long-term shift to the principle of insurance for long-term needs? I will address such issues later in this chapter.

An Office of National Statistics (ONS) Lifestyle Survey has pointed to a number of striking changes over the past four decades:

- The proportion of one-parent families has increased from 8% to 22% with all the attendant problems of stress from family breakdown and also poverty and numbers on benefits.
- The number of single person households has increased from 2% to 10% and reflects not only those who are widowed but also young people living on their own.
- The number of smokers has been cut from 45% to 20% and reductions in alcohol consumption have also been reported.
- Nevertheless, the UK has very high levels of obesity with all the attendant problems to health and early deaths.
- In 1971 only two-fifths of households had a telephone whereas in 2011 virtually every household had.
- In the forty years since the Divorce Reform Act of 1969 Britain has had the highest divorce rate in Europe but it is claimed that as a result people worked through to happier marriages.

A BBC documentary three years ago suggested that in the 'noughties' (2000s) there had been a shift from class war to the war of the generations. The programme drew attention to the 'Age of Kidulthood' and the concerns with ageing, with wars on wrinkles, Botox parties, and the middle aged in denial of their loss of youth. In recent decades there has been the emergence of a celebrity culture which has challenged traditional values and statuses. At times this had led to the stereotyping of those living on council estates as 'chavs'. But the high incomes paid to celebrities such as footballers demonstrated that luxury was no longer the prerogative of the posh. This trend is reflected in consumerist trends such as designer bags with logos, sold with huge mark-ups and proclaiming: 'I've arrived; I'm here and I'm comfortably off.' A recent interview with a Chinese tourist, one of the new upwardly mobile, made the point quite explicitly in spite of saying it under the statue of Karl Marx! Consumerism is a global phenomenon encouraged by the present dominance of de-regulated liberal capitalism and the supremacy of market forces in decision-making. Career ladders no longer exist and there is a myth that success is accessible to all. The prominence of the celebrity class has fooled people into thinking we are a meritocratic society where all the top jobs are open to the talented. The reality is that access to professional jobs remains biased to those privileged through education.

One of the matters which is likely to cause you particular concern is the matter of housing. Do you aspire to own your own home? Would you be able to get a mortgage and put down an appropriate initial deposit? Would you be happy renting? Before you dismiss this possibility it is worth recalling just how relatively recent the shift from renting to owner-occupation has been in the UK. 100 years ago only one in ten homes were privately owned; most were rented from private landlords.

In the post-war years there was a huge expansion of local authority housing and by 1970 nearly one-third of the housing stock was under local authority control. But in the 1980s the Government introduced a 'right-to-buy' scheme and local authorities were discouraged from building new council houses. Consequently there has been a massive decline in the stock of council homes. The numbers renting from local authorities was 32% thirty years ago but has now declined to around 18%. There have been other significant changes in the past few years. Thus owner-occupation, either outright or with a mortgage, peaked at 71% in 2003 but declined to 66% in 2010/11. By the end of the twentieth century the privately rented sector had declined to around 10% but in recent years there has been a resurgence as there is a national shortage of affordable housing.

For many years house building rates have been lower than the demand. They peaked in 1968 when there were 426,000 completions. But this declined to around 200,000 a year from the early 1980s and 137,400 in 2010-11. The consequence was a massive 'housing bubble' as the older generation benefitted from high levels of house inflation. But like all bubbles, it burst when banks realised they had over-stretched themselves and there was the credit crunch from 2007/8 and a financial crisis which has now lasted five years and looks certain to be with us for another decade or more.

So where does this leave you, especially if you have incurred a large debt at university, and if you are struggling to obtain stable employment with reasonable prospects of advancement, and nourish a long-term relationship with someone you would like to marry?

5. *Reform of the Welfare State*

Given the scale of Britain's debt and recent frantic attempts to reduce it by savage cuts in welfare benefits, it is perhaps not unsurprising that some commentators are interpreting current plans as part of a systematic attempt to dismantle the welfare state as it has grown in the post-war years. One of the key principles of the Welfare State as originally conceived was that of 'universalism', that all citizens were entitled to the same treatment whatever their individual circumstances. Today, for example, every pensioner is entitled to a free bus pass and in principle, treatment in the NHS is free for all. But as we noted above, there are major demographic changes taking place and expectations for improved services are ever upwards while technological advances are very costly. Inevitably, demands exceed current resources. In the past prescription and dental charges were first introduced. In the future it is difficult to see how some sort of rationing and selection between alternative possibilities will not be inevitable. The current wild talk about 'strivers' and 'skivers' has created a climate of opinion which is sometimes hostile to the underlying principles of the welfare state such as providing a safety net for all those in need, the poor, deprived, unemployed, homeless, and so on. What is likely to be the future of the NHS?

A related issue is the matter of the care of the elderly, especially those who require long-term care. As I noted above, the projections are startling: there are likely to be very big increases in the number of people aged over 65 within 15-20 years and the incidence of the five most chronic conditions among them is predicted to increase by between one quarter and one half and cost nearly one quarter of the NHS budget. How will this be paid for and who will pay? Your generation will have to pick up whatever mess our generations leave you with and will have to decide how important the principle of universalism is, that every citizen has an equal worth and right to treatment. Or does it depend, for example, on the area of need or support? Should the principle hold for, say, appendicitis, pneumonia and cancer but not for obesity, drug addiction or for cosmetic treatments?

In 2011 the Commission on Funding of Care and Support under the chairmanship of Andrew Dilnot reported to the

Government. It highlighted that the current funding system was in urgent need of reform because it was difficult to understand, often unfair and unsustainable and left some people exposed to potentially catastrophic care costs and no way to protect themselves. There were two main recommendations. First, an individual's contribution towards *social care costs* (not including bed and breakfast or 'hotel' costs) should be capped around £35,000. Second, the means-tested threshold above which people are liable for their full care costs should be increased to £100,000. The Government recently announced plans to cap care costs at £75,000 to be largely met from the introduction of the flat rate state pension as well as extending the current freeze on inheritance tax.

Commenting on the proposed reform the Joseph Rowntree Foundation interpreted it as a sharing of the costs in later life between individuals and the state with individuals paying for their own care costs, which are currently potentially unlimited, until they reach a 'cap' after which the state pays for their care. In other words, this is a 'limited liability' model of social insurance. The proposal was intended to make the system feel much fairer for large numbers of home-owners.

Well, I don't know what you think but I certainly found the whole matter incredibly complicated and difficult to follow. But the main point is that a proportion of elderly people, usually parents, will need to spend some time in residential care in their later years. Who should pay for this and how should it be paid for? Do we expect it to be paid for by the state out of taxes or should we all cover for unanticipated future needs by means of insurance all through our lives? In principle, why should it be expected by children that they will inherit a large endowment on their parents' deaths in the way of their parents' savings and property accumulation? How much of a 'right' do we have to an inheritance?

Given the dysfunctionality of our present society, and indeed of the world, is it not time to reconsider the principles of social welfare? There seems to be a growing consensus that a serious overhaul is necessary, and, to use a phrase from the famous Beveridge Report, that this is a 'revolutionary' moment. Yet the sad fact is that at the moment, on the evidence of the parliamentary debate on 8 January 2013, our politicians are involved in a party points-scoring contest rather than a serious national effort to seek a revolutionary new and more appropriate model of social welfare suitable for the long-term needs of our country in a globalised world. The outcome will have serious consequences for your long-term welfare.

Will Hutton recently wrote an article entitled 'It's not too late to make Britain a good place in which to grow old'. Referring to the Dilnot Report on planning for the care of the elderly, he contrasted the policies of 'low tax individualism' where each individual has total responsibility to ensure they are adequately prepared for their retirement years, and 'social risk pooling' where the risks of illness and disability are shared by everyone through national insurance or taxation. Three options were suggested: (a) raising funds from general taxation; (b) divert spending from other areas; or (c) raise funds by taxing the over-65s. None of these options would be popular. Hutton went on to argue, in my view correctly, 'that the best way of delivering *risk pooling* is social insurance', that is increased national insurance or taxation. This would be pragmatic, show solidarity to those at risk (always unknown), recognise the equal dignity of all citizens, and demonstrate a concern to promote the common good. What do you think?

6. Concluding Reflections

You may have found the outline I have presented in this letter about domestic realities in the UK depressing and shocking. Perhaps that is no bad thing. As I write shortly before Easter 2013 there is a great deal of pessimism about the state of the

UK economy. The current depression is the longest ever recorded, longer even than those of the 1920s and 1930s. This is the world into which you will be journeying through adulthood. I suggest that you need to be realistic about it and set out on your own journey with guts and commitment. With this in mind let us recap some of the issues which you will have to face and determine what you want to do about them.

- ***Deficit and Debt: Living within your Means:*** Firstly, we sketched the basic facts about the UK's annual budget deficit and accumulated debt. The current government is attempting to get to grips with these matters but it is clearly a global issue and the UK cannot overlook what is happening in the rest of the world and especially Europe. Nevertheless, it is important that you think about a sort of national addiction to debt. It has become a sort of cultural habit to borrow for purchases and pay for them by credit card. Do you think this has been a good model for ordinary people and have you thought about starting to save regularly? If you expect one day to take out a mortgage on a house have you considered what sort of deposit the building society or bank will expect you to put down initially? Do you approve of the idea of 'conspicuous consumption', that is demonstrating your success by purchasing the most glamorous purchases with designer labels and so on? Will that be helpful if you are scrimping around trying to bring up a family on a modest income?

- ***Employment Trends:*** Secondly, we reviewed some of the many changes which have taken place in recent years in the distribution of employment. In my lifetime we have seen huge reductions in the numbers employed in agriculture, mining and manufacturing and a major shift from heavy engineering to new technologies and sciences such as pharmaceuticals. Apart from these sector shifts there has also been a cultural shift so that increasing numbers of women are now in the labour market. A sign of the times has been the big increase in part-time employment and also of the numbers who are self-employed. Both these trends probably reflect the uncertain prospects for the economy but also the striving for maximum labour market flexibility which has been driven by government policies since the 1980s. These were intended to generate more creativity, invention and innovation and so contribute to a more robust economy. Finally, the new information and communication technologies have revolutionised our world over the past two or three decades. They have offered great possibilities but we also noted concerns such as the concentration of power by the state or large commercial organisations. Where do you expect or intend to fit into this new world of employment with all its uncertainties?

- ***Poverty and Inequality:*** Thirdly, we had a look at some of the nasty aspects of our present society such as poverty and high and increasing levels of inequality. At the present time I suggest we need to be discomforted by the fact that it is the poorest people who seem to be hit hardest by government policies of cuts and austerity in seeking benefits cuts when it was not the poor who were responsible for the economic mess the world has been in since 2007. I suggested that talk about 'scroungers' and 'skivers' was not helpful and was indeed a highly misleading myth. The struggles of poor people deserve a more honest understanding and sympathetic consideration. Particularly striking was the evidence that increasing inequality is related to a whole range of social ills including shorter life expectancy and higher levels of a wide range of illnesses. I reported some of the evidence about inequality in the UK and suggest it remains a major challenge to our social consciences.

- ***Demographic Trends:*** Fourthly, we reviewed some of the recent demographic changes and the changing nature of our family structures. There is a great deal more we could have considered, such as increasing cohabitation, high divorce rates, and ethnic composition and recent migration trends, but they were not so central to the concerns of this book. What did seem important to note was the incredible rise in the average life expectancy of people in the UK and the projections for huge increases in the numbers of the elderly with corresponding pressures on pensions and the provision of care. The evidence suggests strongly that there is a serious need for revolutionary changes– rather than reformist tinkering – about how these new demands will be paid for. That means we, now, and you, in the future, will need to have an honest look at such issues as the universality of state benefits such as health care and pensions and methods of paying for them when everything points to much longer retirement lives. Finally, I raised the issue of housing and noted recent trends which reflect increasing difficulties in entering the owner-occupied sector of the housing market. This is a major change from a generation ago and has not been helped by a woefully poor house building programme year after year.

- ***The Future of the Welfare State:*** Fifthly, we considered the reform of the Welfare State and issues such as pensions and long-term care of the elderly and how these are to be paid for when the numbers of those over 65 is increasing so rapidly. Are our national insurance contributions adequate or realistic? Should the state pay and, if so, should there be an equalitarian provision based on the concepts of 'social risk pooling' and 'universalism'? Or should we accept a 'low tax individualism' which puts the entire responsibility onto the individual person so that if they fail to make sufficient provision for their old age that is their hard luck? Seven decades ago Beveridge introduced a 'revolutionary moment' into our system of social security and the Welfare State as we have known it was born. Do you think that the time has come to introduce a new revolutionary overhaul of the Welfare State, including the NHS?

In sum, this letter has tried to identify some key aspects of the domestic realities in the UK today just as the previous letter looked at some key global realities facing you today. In Part II of this book I will attempt to provide a social analysis of what we have identified so far. Letter 4 will reflect on the nature of the form of liberal capitalism which has emerged as dominant in our world today while Letter 5 will aim to discern where the main sources of power are and who it is that in the last analysis has the power of decision-making and choice.

Part II

Social Analysis

Letter 4

Power Relationships

In Part II of this book I will offer a social analysis of the problems and issues we noted in Part I. In this letter I will discuss the nature of power relationships of various types in a globalising world while in Letter 5 I will explore the possibilities of countervailing forces such as the United Nations and its various agencies, regional collaboration such as the European Union, international financial agencies such as the International Monetary Fund and the World Bank, and communitarian efforts to improve the fairness of development in the southern half of the world. Again I will aim to use accessible language and, where relevant, draw on contemporary issues in the news.

1. The Nature of Social Power

One of the obvious conclusions from the two previous letters is that the world is not characterised by fairness. There are clearly structural injustices which result from the differential power of decision-making between the rich and the poor, people as well as nations, and the ability of the powerful to determine the rules of the game, such as taxation and welfare policies, immigration rules and restrictions, trade regulations, favoured groups, corporations, nations or institutional arrangements. What is the nature of power which enables these huge inequalities and injustices to persist? Essentially power is the possibility of imposing one's will despite the resistance of others. But it also includes what might be called the 'mobilisation of bias', for example by means of a monopoly of the mass media or a totalitarian state such as North Korea. It can also include the control of agendas and the consideration of what is important and what not so that awkward issues are simply ignored.

As I was beginning to gather my thoughts for the writing of this letter I came across an advert for a new book by Michael Mann entitled *The Sources of Social Power*. His newly published fourth volume deals with the post-war period of globalisation. He defines power as 'the capacity to get others to do things that otherwise they would not do'. He points out that power 'may be collective, embodying cooperation to achieve shared goals – power through others – and distributive, wielded by some over others.' This is not just theoretical but reflects the world in which you will grow up and have to cope with.

Mann goes on helpfully to suggest there are four types of power which you will face on your journey through life. First, there is what he calls *ideological power* which he suggests 'derives from the human need to find ultimate meaning in life, to share norms and values... with others.' He sees ideologies as 'the search for ultimate meaning in the interplay of military, political, and economic power relations.' In recent years we have had communism, fascism and social democracy. As we shall discuss later claims such as 'there is no alternative' to free, unregulated markets, or liberal capitalism are contemporary ideologies which frame the way people look at things and come to decisions. Other examples would include feminist ideologies about the systemic exclusion of women in patriarchal societies or secularist ideologies which reject any sort of religious dimension to life. I would also argue that the tabloid press systematically distort issues and imply that 'one off' cases are typical of the world we live in. Usually this means the stigmatising of particular minority groups like asylum seekers, or the unemployed as 'shirkers'.

Second, there is *economic power* 'which derives from the human need to extract, transform, distribute, and consume the product of nature'. At the present time capitalism is the globally dominant type of economic transaction treating 'all the means of production, including labour, as commodities'. There are four main types of markets: for capital, labour, production and consumption. Seeking high profits becomes more important than seeking the common good or equitable distribution. Mann suggests that in recent times capitalism has been 'the most consistently dynamic power organisation... responsible for most technological innovation (but also for) most environmental degradation.' Included here is the huge power of multinational corporations to influence political and economic decision-making both in this country and internationally.

Third, there is *military power* which Mann defines as 'the social organisation of concentrated and lethal violence.' It is 'most lethally wielded by the armed forces of states in interstate wars, though paramilitaries, guerrillas, and terrorists will all figure.' While there may be close links with political and economic power, the military are often a distinct group in society with independent power to control life. This might obviously be the case in countries like Burma and North Korea but let us not forget that it was an American President who complained about the decision-making power of the 'military-industrial complex' even in a democratic society.

Fourth is *political power* which Mann sees as 'the centralised and territorial regulation of social life'. Networks of political power are routinely organised around a territorial and centralised state. In democratic societies political power is periodically expressed through regular elections of candidates from different parties such as the Conservative, Liberal

Democrat and Labour parties in the UK or the Democrats and Republicans in the US. In spite of rhetoric about freedom and local autonomy in this country, for example through County Councils, in practice the central state keeps a very tight control over their finances. Special interest groups and campaigning groups and non-governmental organisations (NGOs) endeavour to influence political decision-making by mobilising public opinion.

As we explore power relationships both domestically and internationally in the first quarter of the twenty-first century it will be helpful to bear in mind the four types Mann has distinguished. But first let us consider how power relations have changed in recent decades.

2. Historical Changes since the 1980s

The Old Testament in the Bible is full of massive historical changes in the distribution of power between a series of empires. Israel had to cope successively with Assyrians, Babylonians, Persians, Macedonians and Romans in the thousand years before Christ. At the end of the eighteenth century the English historian Edward Gibbon famously wrote *The History of the Decline and Fall of the Roman Empire.* When I first went to school in the late 1930s we gloated over the fact that half the globe was painted red; that was the British Empire. But it is no more; it declined and fell in the post-World War II years. In my lifetime I have also witnessed the decline and fall of the Nazi 'empire' in Europe in the mid-1940s and the decline and fall of Soviet forms of communism in Eastern Europe in the late 1980s. From that period there has been only one 'superpower', the United States. But all the current evidence suggests that within a decade or so, the US will be supplanted by the rising power of China and possibly the other BRIC countries. It is, perhaps, important that you realise that the world you are experiencing today is likely to change dramatically in your lifetimes.

In 1992 Francis Fukuyama, an American political scientist, famously wrote a book entitled *The End of History and the Last Man* in which he argued that the progression of human history as a struggle between ideologies, such as communism and capitalism, is largely at an end with the world settling on liberal democracy. He predicted the eventual global triumph of political and economic liberalism and wrote: 'what we may be witnessing is not just the end of the Cold War, or the passing of a particular period of post-war history, but the end of history as such. That is, the end of mankind's ideological evolution and the universalisation of Western liberal democracy as the final form of human government.' Fukuyama was also active in the infamous 'Project for the New American Century' think tank. This reflected a form of US and Western triumphalism which, of course, has been strongly challenged in subsequent decades. In fairness it should be said that Fukuyama did modify his analysis later but he argued that the threat of radical Islam after the 9/11 terrorist attacks had been overstated and that the negative attitude of the US government towards the UN and other inter-governmental organisations was likely to increase anti-Americanism in other parts of the world.

So what can we say about changes in the distribution of power since the collapse of communism in Eastern Europe in the late 1980s? I suggest that the first thing we can say is that the pretentions of US power, certainly military but also as we shall discuss later, economic have been shown to be over optimistic. Not many would argue that the Iraq war was a success, and in many ways, the country is currently ravaged by sectarian conflict. The same goes for the war in Afghanistan. It is by no means certain that a strong government will emerge which will reconcile the different tribes and safeguard the advances made by women. Future conflict within Afghanistan seems highly likely. Furthermore, it could be argued that the so-called 'war on terror' has in fact mobilised pro-jihadist Moslems against the US and the West more generally, for example in Mali. Recent bombings in Boston and Nairobi and successful prosecutions and preventions of planned attacks by young men brought up in this country are timely reminders that US, and more generally western military power and intelligence are not necessarily sufficient to prevent deadly attacks.

There also seems to be a potentially dangerous spread of nuclear capabilities in spite of international attempts to limit them. Israel, India, Pakistan and China are now nuclear powers and both Iran and North Korea defiantly aim to develop their own nuclear capabilities. It is one of the issues which your generation will have to face over the next few decades. My point is that traditional military superiority seems unlikely to guarantee peace and security where there are small, ideologically driven fanatics prepared to cause terror in pursuing their aims or to protest against long-standing relationships or injustices. In the following letter we will consider some of the countervailing forces seeking reconciliation between competing powers. The two letters in Part III will look at the contribution which a Catholic faith can bring to the negotiating table.

3. The Implications of New Cyber Technology

In this section I would like to address a subject with which your generation is much more at ease than oldies like me. It is only in the past two or three decades that computers and information and communication technology have become part of everyday life. You find it natural to surf the web or look up things on Google or text your friends with instant messages. People of my generation joke about having to consult their grandchildren about anything to do with computers. You may have no fears about on-line banking, shopping or purchasing through Amazon. People of my generation, on the other hand, are highly suspicious of 'Big Brother' possibilities, identities being stolen, and so on. Today, for example, BT threatened that if I do not pay for their services online they will charge £1.50 to send their bill by post. I recently watched a programme in which Google offered to put all the books in major university libraries, including Harvard and Oxford, in digital form so that everyone would have free access to them. At first the libraries felt this was performing a public service until an organised group of authors obtained legal protection of their rights under copyright laws when it became clear that their work was being sold for profit. So the purpose of this section is to explore some of the implications, pros and cons, of the relatively new information technology.

Three items in the news over the weekend that I started to draft this section indicated some of the significance of these relatively new developments. First of all a false story of two explosions in the White House and that Barack Obama had been injured posted on Twitter resulted in a sudden fall in the stock market. Just over two minutes later the story was denied and the stock market regained its original valuations. This indicates not only the instant nature of communications world-wide these days but also the potential harm that can be done by a remote attack. Secondly, when we visited our nearly three year old granddaughter she was dancing around with a little Leap Pad selecting and singing her favourite tunes. This reminded me of an article in the weekend paper written by a mother of three young children all struggling with their iPads and related gadgets. She reported the case of a four year old who had been using an iPad for four hours a day and been having compulsive behaviour therapy. Teenagers spend hours texting and social networking on Facebook and Twitter. But researchers have reported that a 'cyber-lifestyle' is 'rewiring our brains' and reduces the ability to read and engage with more sophisticated concepts and analysis. Thirdly, there was a report that some well-known food companies were avoiding the bans on television advertising by showing questionable material on their own child-friendly websites. For example, the Swizzles Town feature aimed at pre-school and primary age children where the player could collect cola bottle sweets was considered irresponsibly to have encouraged an unhealthy lifestyle. A fourth example of new developments is the use of Skype to engage in face-to-face communication with relatives who may have emigrated to Australia or New Zealand. Such technological developments which have emerged in recent years are transforming our lives and relationships globally. It is worth reflecting on this new information and communication technology and at least raising the issues of who controls these developments and what power do they have over our lives.

The origins of the internet, which is 'a worldwide publicly accessible system of interconnected computer networks', go back to the development of electronic computers in the 1950s. When I started lecturing in 1959 there was a computer which completely filled a somewhat mysterious room in the college. How rapidly miniaturisation has proceeded in the past half-century. It was as recently as 1989 that Tim Berners-Lee, a computer scientist, invented the World Wide Web which is 'a system of interlinked hypertext documents accessed via the Internet.' While the Internet is 'a global system of interconnected computer networks', the web can be seen as 'an application running on the internet.' Wikipedia is helpful in making these distinctions though I cannot say I fully understand them. There are currently over two billion web users. Of some concern is the danger to personal privacy of on-line bullies on social networking sites who may make use of personal information to harass marginal or stigmatised individuals. Identity theft, fraud, espionage and intelligence gathering are all types of cybercrime. Since I first drafted this paragraph there has been considerable debate about the surveillance activities of GCHQ in the UK and the NSA in the US. What is the proper balance between national security and personal privacy?

Wikipedia suggests there is some disagreement among computer programmers about the definition of 'hacker'. But a useful starting point is that 'in the computer security context, a hacker is someone who seeks and exploits weaknesses in a computer system or computer network.' They may be 'motivated by... profit, protest or challenge'. One example of the protest type is Wikileaks which sees itself as 'an international, online, non-profit organisation which publishes secret information, news leaks, and classified media from anonymous sources.' It claims to be 'of assistance to peoples of all countries who wish to reveal unethical behaviour in their governments and institutions... (and aims) for maximum political impact.' Various governments were embarrassed when secret messages relating to the Iraq War and international relations were reported by Wikileaks. This is a good example of the powerful being exposed to challenge by deviant countervailing forces when existing channels of debate and exposure have not been effective in democratic societies. It is clearly an area where there is likely to be further debate in the future. The powerful, whether governments, political leaders involved in delicate negotiations, the military concerned about security issues, or commercial interests preferring to keep their profit-seeking endeavours firmly under wraps, all have an interest in controlling debate. It remains a more open question as to whether that is in the interests of people generally or the common good.

Another controversial term is 'cyberterrorism' which can be defined as 'the intentional use of computer networks and public internet to cause disruption and harm' for political or ideological reasons. As 2000 approached there was much concern about the 'millennium bug' and an awareness of the potential of cyber terrorism. It has been suggested that we have not yet devised appropriate institutions to manage the huge and rapid advances which have been made in information technology and communications and a number of states, including China and Israel, have set up elite units to defend vital infrastructure networks.

In this section I have attempted to indicate the importance of the new technologies which have been developed with incredible speed over the past few decades. It seems likely that they will become increasingly important in your own lives. They will open up information transfer and communication opportunities which far surpass anything available to my generation. But as with all human developments, they can be used for good purposes and to promote the common good globally, or they can be used by powerful groups and institutions to control and manipulate ordinary people. It will be up to you to make appropriate judgements about policies for their successful regulation.

4. The Dominance of Free Market Capitalism

In this section I propose to explore the area of economic power, the ability to determine the way the economy and financial arrangements work. To put it crudely, when Soviet Communism collapsed in Russia and in Eastern Europe in the late 1980s, it was attributed to the long-term superiority of the freedom of the market and of individuals to exploit it for profit over the attempt by totalitarian states to control every aspect of economic life, what, where and how much was produced and how and to whom the products were distributed. It seemed that capitalism had 'won'. But as Will Hutton pointed out some time ago, there are numerous forms of capitalism: the Anglo-American form of de-regulated 'liberal' capitalism (which he calls American conservatism), the social-democratic forms in Western Europe, and more recently, the state form of capitalism in China and other East Asian countries.

In the 1980s both Reagan in the US and Thatcher in the UK de-regulated the markets. As I have written elsewhere, while both the 'American Conservatism' and 'European Social Market' forms of capitalism (to use Hutton's terms) share a commitment to democracy, human rights and market capitalism, there are major differences in their core values and goals. American Conservatism was driven by a belief in uncontrolled individualism and a minimalist state. The *rights* of ownership took precedence over *duties* to share. Individual success was seen as the reward for hard work and virtue so that minimal obligations to the poor and needy were acknowledged. The public realm and need for some sort of social contract were barely considered. (As I revise this paragraph, this can be seen clearly in the drama of the shutdown of some federal state activities in the United States as a result of intransigent Republican opposition to the Obama health care reforms.) Social welfare was regarded as an individual responsibility and public provision was minimal. In the UK successive governments from Thatcher, through Blair and Brown, to Cameron and Osborne, and in the US, Republicanism, have to a large extent followed American conservative economics, the pursuit of flexible labour markets, constraints on trade union activity and the privatisation of public services.

The European Social Market was premised on quite different values. The security and prosperity of the community as a whole and social justice concerns promoted by a facilitative and cooperative state were valued. The wealthy were regarded as having obligations towards the less fortunate and the need for a social contract between different stakeholders, such as shareholders and trade unionists, was regarded as essential for the cohesion of society. The public realm was salient for this reason and citizenship values and communitarian collaboration were important. While it is right to consider critically the social implications of neo-liberal capitalism and see it as the cause of the commodification of people's lives and of many of the problems and injustices we noted in Part I, it is only proper to recognise some of its advantages. As one commentator has put it, 'capitalism is a growth machine' which has resulted in huge increases in living standards and improved shelter, health, mortality and morbidity standards for an increasing number of people over recent decades. But it is clear that the current form of Anglo-American liberal capitalism has seen very significant increases in inequality both within societies such as our own and internationally between the developed and less-developed societies.

Let us now consider some of the implications of globalisation. Increasing trade and competition in the global market place has had major consequences for the distribution of power. Since the 1980s when Reagan and Thatcher de-regulated financial markets and squeezed workers' rights in order to introduce greater flexibility for employers and reduce labour costs there has been a downward squeeze on the proportion of output going to pay labour costs. Cheap labour in developing societies has led profit-driven commercial enterprises to 'outsource' to them. One obvious example is that any telephone query to any of our energy companies is usually answered by someone in the Indian sub-continent. Other examples of the consequences of international competition include the collapse of much of our manufacturing sector and the growth of the financial sector following de-regulation. The largest companies all strive to have a global reach with branches in countries all over the world.

One consequence of the ascendancy of neo-liberal capitalism has been the growth of consumerism. The imperative urge to buy goods beyond what can be afforded currently has been fuelled by the rapid rise of both personal and national debt. This led to the collapse of the sub-prime housing market in the US in 2007 and subsequently to the global recession which we are still experiencing, and the acute economic difficulties being faced by countries such as Greece and Spain. Michael Mann argues that this phase of development has now reached the more successful economies in the Southern hemisphere. Countries such as China, India and Brazil are rapidly growing economically, encouraged by international institutions such as the International Monetary

Fund and the World Bank which are largely dominated by the prevailing orthodoxy of neo-liberal capitalist thinking. This has encouraged the expansion of western commercial interests but has also provided a model which is increasingly being adopted by the developing BRIC nations.

If I were to offer a suggestion for your own children it would be to learn Chinese. China has for a decade or so experienced extremely rapid growth rates and it is interesting to note that China now provides the largest group of tourists worldwide. As has previously been mentioned, China is expected to become the world's largest economy within the next decade or so. This clearly indicates the changing power relationships in the world. Slowly, but quite definitely, the traditional supremacy of the west, and more particularly the US and Europe, is being threatened by the steady rise of the major nations of the Southern hemisphere. This seems likely to become an everyday reality in your own lifetimes. As they go through the phase of industrialisation they are likely to require huge increases of energy, mainly from fossil fuels. This is likely to produce its own tensions, and a major challenge to attempts to combat climate change. The urgent need for a collaborative international response to the challenge of climate change will be considered further in Letter 5.

In sum, the current distribution of *economic power* reflects the dominance of a neo-liberal form of capitalism though different versions are to be found for example in China. From the early 1980s neo-liberal forms of capitalism which were first promoted by Thatcher in the UK and Reagan in the US and have been aggressively pursued by succeeding governments. Internationally neo-liberal forms of capitalism have been promoted by the major economic institutions such as the IMF and the World Bank which have been dominated by western, and especially US commercial interests. Militarily, as we have noted, it is to be hoped that inter-state rivalries will become more regulated and reconciled. It seems unlikely that the current dominance of US *military power* will continue as much larger states such as China and India continue to grow. It is to be hoped that terrorist activity will increasingly prompt international efforts of inter-state collaboration. In spite of the democratic nature of the UK and western nations generally, *political power* has been substantially manipulated by mass media which are largely controlled by those representing commercial and financial interests. In this country, for example, the way that public opinion has been formed by horror stories about the European Union or the scapegoating of welfare 'scroungers' and 'skivers' is frightening. Internationally, the power which the US, and more widely major western nations, currently exercise for example through the United Nations Security Council, is likely to decline steadily as the rising BRIC nations flex their own economic, ideological, military and political muscles and demand more representative international institutions which reflect their own interests more. *Ideologically*, the prevalence of English as a global language and the dominance of Hollywood and other western media, music and entertainment is clear. However, as the nations of the southern hemisphere develop their economic power and corresponding political power, it is increasingly likely that the cultural norms of the South, including religious understandings of the meaning of life, will challenge the current dominance of western ideas, secularism, and culture generally.

This brief review has suggested that we live at a time when the ideology and practice of neo-liberal economics substantially dominate our lives both in this country and globally. It is powerfully promoted by the US throughout the world and is reflected in the exercise of political power by national and international institutions. To adapt a remark once made by President Eisenhower, there is a very influential industrial, economic, commercial, and military complex which exercises power throughout the world. This is subject to challenge and possibly even change as the developing nations of the southern hemisphere begin to counter the current power of the west.

5. The Challenge of Climate Change

There is little doubt that the world is substantially dominated by economic and financial interests which favour and encourage the adoption of neo-liberal capitalism as if there was no alternative. Political leadership even in democratic societies often seems strangled by short-term concerns and the winning of the next election. Even the 'most powerful man on earth', Barack Obama, is often frustratingly constrained by Republican market fundamentalists. Long-term planning is almost invariably unpopular because it often requires the diversion of resources or the discomfort of transport dislocation. There are numerous examples of this such as the procrastination over decades about the building of new airport runways or high-speed rail links or the maintenance of underground railway lines. Another example would be the procrastination by governments over many decades over the making of better pension provision for a population which is living far longer than ever before by demanding more realistic national insurance contributions.

Similarly, difficult international problems are not addressed because they would result in some discomfort for individual states or their populations or powerful commercial interests. The most obvious example of this is that of climate change as a result of global warming caused largely by the burning of fossil fuels since the start of the industrial revolution in western societies in the nineteenth century. Remarkably, the nations of the world did achieve agreement over the danger to the earth's ozone layer after serious holes were found in the 1970s with the danger of excessive ultraviolet radiation resulting in alarming increases of skin cancers. After the US government had taken action to ban man-made halocarbon refrigerants such as chlorofluorocarbons (CFCs) in 1976, the worldwide concern led to the adoption of the Montreal Protocol in 1987 which banned the production of CFCs and other ozone-depleting chemicals. This was subsequently strengthened in London and Copenhagen in spite of considerable resistance from governments in Germany, France and the UK defending the interests of their chemical industries.

But the longer-term issue of global warming still has not generated the same commitments. Governments have been more preoccupied since 2007 with coping with the recession and with stimulating economic growth and managing high levels of debt. Since the early years of the twentieth century the Earth's mean surface temperature has increased by about 0.8°C, with two-thirds of the increase since 1980. Climate model projections are for a further increase of 2-6°C during the 21st century. These increases are caused primarily by such human activities as the burning of fossil fuels, such as coal and oil, and extensive deforestation. The effects of this warming have become increasingly apparent with the melting of the polar icecaps, rising sea levels, changing patterns of rainfall, a probable expansion of subtropical deserts, for example in Africa, extreme weather conditions, and threats to food production and security. Some predictions estimate well over 100 million refugees as a result of rising sea levels in low-lying countries such as Bangladesh.

In his analysis of the four types of social power Michael Mann concludes by looking at the two global crises: the neo-liberal recession and climate change. As he aptly observes: 'climate change (is) generated by our own supposed mastery over nature, humanity's peak of collective power... (It) has been created by capitalism ably assisted by both nation-states and individual consuming citizens... The climate knows no national boundaries. It is global.' There no longer seems to be any scientific doubt that 'environmental degradation (is) threatening the destruction of humanity.' In 2005 the heads of eleven national academies of science, including those of the US, the UK and all four BRIC countries wrote to the G8 heads of government warning that global climate change was 'a clear and increasing threat.' In 2007 in the UK the Stern Review predicted that a 5°C rise in temperatures was a distinct possibility in the twenty-first century and that annual global emissions of carbon dioxide needed to be reduced by 80% from the 1990 level by 2050 to avoid disaster. Stern considered that 'climate change is the greatest market failure the world has ever seen.'

Yet all the key players are prepared to sweep the problem away for future generations, like yours, to address. Capitalist enterprises, for example coal and oil, insist on the demands of short-term profit and the expectations of consumers for growth and rising living standards. Their lobbying and substantial collaboration with the media industries, massively influences public opinion. Nation-states have short-term electoral demands and seek only to improve the standard of living of their citizens. The UN Climate Change Conference in Copenhagen in 2009, for example, was dominated by the US and China and produced only a non-binding Accord. The larger developing countries such as India and China are in the early stages of industrialisation and do not see why they should introduce controls which the developed societies did not at a similar stage. Individual consumers insist on their rights to more goods and a steadily rising standard of living, preferably today. So the reality is that with the dominance of neo-liberal capitalism, all three major groups of players: commercial enterprises, nation-states, and consumers, all have a distinctly short-term view of the dangers of climate change. The result is prolonged procrastination with a serious global issue beyond the capacity of any one government to address.

Mann concludes pessimistically: 'Greenhouse gas emissions are saturating the atmosphere, the sea and the land of planet Earth. At some point in the twenty-first century if the world does not adopt major mitigating policies, global warming will severely menace human society. It will hit unevenly, poorer countries hardest, but it will also reduce living standards everywhere.' You have been warned!

6. Conclusion: The Global Context of Your Lives

The main purpose of this letter has been to analyse why it is that the distributions of social outcomes, both domestic and international, are so wretchedly unequal. It has been suggested that the answer is to be found in the massive inequalities of social power: economic, political, cultural and military. Coordination of these different types of social power results from the global dominance since the collapse of the Soviet empire in the late 1980s of neo-liberal capitalism. It is the central link in explaining the way the world is at this moment in time. It has managed to persuade the world that 'there is no alternative' or better way to run the economy. Commercial enterprises are only too pleased to concur while the political leaders of democratic nation states provide legitimacy and support to them in return for the growth and improved standards of living they generate for their ever-demanding and consumerist populations.

The evidence of the past few years, especially since the financial crisis of 2007, has demonstrated the power of major commercial enterprises, banks, financial institutions and large producers of global wealth. It is not disgraced bankers or the wealthy who have suffered the consequences of the recent financial crisis but the poor and those struggling to make ends meet who have lost their jobs and often their homes. Capitalist enterprises all have an interest in maximising short-term profits and growth at virtually any cost, such as dodgy factory buildings in Bangladesh. One of the consequences of the huge differentials in economic power is that it operates overwhelmingly in the interests of the wealthy. Since the deregulation promoted by Thatcher and Reagan in the 1980s there have been steep rises in inequality both in the UK and US, and internationally between the developed and developing countries.

Political power in the UK, and generally in the democratic west, substantially operates in support of the economic interests of capitalist institutions. It seems clear that the failure to introduce a more thorough and binding regulatory system for the banks five or six years after the banking crisis reflects the hidden power of financial interests. In a similar way the cynical cutting of benefits to the poor while reducing tax rates for the richest people suggests that economic power is to a considerable extent reflected in political decisions. Governments are also constrained by their short-term interests in winning the next election. Their electors are primarily seen as consumers who have been led to expect continuing economic growth and rising levels of living standards. Hence they feel constrained to promote policies in the economic interests of consumers.

There was an appropriate comment made in the *Guardian* on the day I completed this letter: 'Governments today have no vision but endless economic growth. They are judged not by the number of people in employment – let alone by the number of people in satisfying, pleasurable jobs – and not by the happiness of the population or the protection of the natural world. Job-free, world-eating growth is fine, as long as it's growth. There are no ends any more, just means.' That sums it up nicely and is a real challenge if your focus should be on ends or goals such as reduced inequalities and the common good.

Cultural power is manifest in the promotion of neo-classical capitalism as self-evident with there being 'no alternative'. I hope you will grow up to be critical of the misleading and sometimes mendacious portrayals offered by the mass media, and especially the tabloid press. The characterisations of huge classes of people as 'skivers and scroungers' or of immigrants, refugees and asylum seekers on the basis of one or two extreme cases is malicious. At the very least you ought to be critical of people who extrapolate beyond the evidence. There seems little doubt that on the whole the influential media largely reflect the ideology of market fundamentalism and also often a nasty streak of xenophobia. As I write this there seem to be good reasons to suspect that the failure to implement the major recommendations of the Leveson Report in the newspaper industry is indicative of the power of economic and media interests to control political decision-making.

Finally, military power in our society can probably be said to reflect the interests of those with political and economic power. It clearly has interests in, for example, extending its capabilities such as the renewal or updating of Trident or the development of more sophisticated drones. There are plenty of economic enterprises which have a special interest in manufacturing the most up-to-date equipment and are only too pleased to obtain lucrative defence contracts.

In sum, all four types of power might be said to have major controlling influences over decision-making in our society, and indeed internationally. But again, the short-termism of economic and political decision makers remains a major weakness. This is best illustrated by the case of climate change and the failure of decision-makers in all the major countries in the world, including the UK and US and the four big BRIC countries to reach a decision on what is arguably the most serious issue facing us all today, with major global implications for the next generation or two, in other words you and your children. But as Michael Mann puts it: 'The bottom line of pessimism (about responding to climate change) is that every government in the world is committed to economic growth.' We might add: 'so are all we consumers!'

I would hope that I have convinced you of the importance in all our lives of the global dimension of power. We live in an increasingly interdependent world. What each of us does will effect everyone else. We need to be aware of the global inequalities in the distribution of power in our world currently dominated by market fundamentalist thinking. In my next letter I will explore the possibilities of promoting countervailing forces to resist and challenge the current inequalities both in our own society and in the world as a whole.

Letter 5

Countervailing Forces

In the previous letter I outlined the various forms of social power: economic, political, cultural and military, which determined the various decisions and social policies of commercial enterprises, nation states and individuals, both of the UK and internationally. In this letter I will explore the possibilities of countervailing forces aiming to control the various forms of social power. These countervailing forces aim to restrict the economic power wielded by wealthy commercial organisations such as banks and multinational corporations (MNCs), and also the nation states they often control and their electors who endeavour to ensure that their interests in improving their standards of living are realised. All three groups tend to dislike any restraints on their choices and self-interests and tend to resist countervailing forces which aim to restrain their powers in the interest of the wider community – both within the nation state and internationally between nations. Unregulated individualism can be divisive and corrosive of social stability and cohesion whereas agreed forms of regulation recognise the need to share and promote the common good and solidarity between all the members of society, whether the nation state or the international community of nation states. In other words, unrestrained individualism needs to be replaced, at least to a substantial degree, by a concern for the common good. In the past this pattern emerged within western, democratic nations; the need now, in this age of globalisation, is to extend the principle internationally.

1. The imperatives of globalisation

Let us first recognise some of the consequences of the globalising tendencies we have observed in recent decades. The UK has historically always been substantially dependent on imported food and raw materials. Since the demise of the coal industry we have been very dependent on oil imports for our energy industries. This explains much of our concern for stability in the Middle East and the oil-producing nations in particular. In recent decades we have lost a great deal of our manufacturing capacity to countries in South East Asia where labour costs have been much lower. If I phone up BT or British Gas (BG) for help or advice I am answered by someone in India. Many such jobs have been 'outsourced' in recent years. If I want a new TV or mobile phone or present for young children, the chances are that they will have been manufactured in China. In other words, we as a nation are totally dependent on the maintenance of supplies and goods from nations across the world.

But the concept of dependence has wider implications. Take, for example, the implications of the financial crisis in Europe. One of the consequences of the Eurozone is that individual states no longer have control over the value of their euro currency. Thus within the past year countries such as Greece, Spain, Cyprus and Italy have been heavily constrained in the running of their own economies and have been very largely dependent on others to facilitate their coping with their substantial difficulties with large annual budget deficits and accumulating debt. The UK is being a little smug in congratulating itself for not having joined the euro. But we are always looking over our shoulders to see whether the various currency rating agencies still regard us as reliable when it comes to the repayment of international loans.

As I drafted this I was reminded of the great poem written by John Donne in 1624. I wrongly attributed it to William Blake but welcome my dependence on Google which put me right!

No Man is an island entire of itself.
Each is a part of the continent, a part of the main.
If a clod be washed away by the sea, Europe is the less.
As well as if a promontory were,
as well as if a manor of thine own or of thy friends were.
Each man's death diminishes me, for I am involved in mankind.
Therefore, send not to know for whom the bell tolls,
It tolls for thee.

I found this reflection and prayer enormously illuminating and to the point. None of us is alone entirely; we are all dependent on others and are part of the whole. It is this sense of interdependence which we must be humble enough to recognise both as individuals and as nations.

As we have noted, globalisation is the process of growing international integration and interdependence arising from the rapid developments in transport, telecommunications including the internet, and all forms of interaction. The International Monetary Fund (IMF) in 2000 identified four basic aspects of globalisation: trade and transactions, capital and investment movements, migration and the movement of people, and the dissemination of knowledge. One commentator has usefully distinguished five dimensions of globalisation: economic, political, cultural, ecological and ideological. Of particular interest is ecological globalisation which includes the worldwide implications of population growth, access to food, the global reduction of biodiversity, increasing inequalities between rich and poor and the global

North and South, human-induced climate change, and global environmental degradation.

Each of these areas tends to be dominated by powerful institutions to a degree which was not the case even in the early post-war years. Take transport, for example. In the early post-war years it used to take a couple of weeks or so to travel from the UK to Australia by sea; now the journey can be completed within a day by air. The developments in communications technology have facilitated the movements of investments and capital virtually instantaneously. Cultural developments facilitated by communications technology include not only transnational aspects of youth culture but also the rapid dissemination of information and ideas, such as were apparent in the so-called Arab Spring. When a child is about to be executed somewhere in the world it instantly gives rise to the mobilisation of concern among ordinary people throughout the world. In sum, the various dimensions of globalisation have made the world a smaller place. We are inevitably more closely connected and interdependent. One of the implications of these globalising imperatives is that we need to recognise our interdependence and seek appropriate means of controlling its various dimensions in the interests of the common good.

In order to respond to the selfishness of uncontrolled individualism or market fundamentalism and the injustices of neo-liberal capitalism we need to recognise our interdependence and learn to share with others in human solidarity and to care for the common good. That is basically what various forms of regulation aim to do, even if we do not recognise it as such.

2. Interdependence and the Weakness of Individual States

One consequence of the recognition by nation states of their individual weakness and need for communal support is the emergence of military alliances to protect against feared rivals. An obvious example here is the North Atlantic Treaty Organisation (NATO) which was signed in 1949 at a time when there appeared to be a serious threat of Soviet expansion into Western Europe. There was a substantial realisation that the countries of North America and Western Europe were mutually interdependent in the defence of western democracy against aggressive Soviet Communism. That threat has substantially disappeared since the collapse of the Soviet empire in Eastern Europe in the late 1980s.

Other examples of the military weakness of individual nation states can perhaps be seen in the cases of Syria, North Korea, Iran and Israel. The longer the conflict in Syria goes on the more complex it becomes. It is no longer simply a case of rebels against a tyrannical dictator but has increasingly become a matter of inter-ethnic and intra-Islamic conflicts with strong inter-state implications and the potential to flare up into a major regional war. This indicates the near-impossibility of an effective intervention by a powerful nation such as the US. Again, while the prospect of states such as North Korea or Iran developing a nuclear capacity is very worrying, nevertheless no state is militarily strong enough to dare intervene. The evidence from the wars in Iraq and Afghanistan over the past decade has also indicated the facile nature of the assumption that military power alone can achieve a satisfactory resolution of conflicts. Finally, no state, even the US, has yet been able to resolve the long-standing conflict between the Israelis and the Palestinians. In sum, no individual nation state is able to impose its will on others by means of military power alone.

The weakness of individual states is also apparent in the economic sphere. A detailed account of the global recession since 2008 would demonstrate the knock-on effects of decisions over which individual states had no control. While this is a highly technical matter, the broad outlines are, I think, apparent. What started as a problem of excessive lending to 'sub-prime' owners in the US housing market led in time to the collapse of Lehman Brothers, the fourth largest investment bank in the US and the largest bankruptcy in US history. This played a major role in the unfolding of the global financial crisis in the late 2000s. Countries around the southern rim of the European Union, such as Greece, were particularly vulnerable and have had to introduce austerity programmes which are politically not only highly unpopular but also potentially likely to result in serious social and political unrest.

In 1992 the UK government experienced a major humiliation on 'Black Wednesday' when it was forced to withdraw the pound sterling from the European Exchange Rate Mechanism (ERM) only two years after it had joined it. They were unable to keep its value above an agreed lower limit and in spite of raising interest rates temporarily to 15% dealers kept selling pounds. The high profile investor and speculator, George Soros, famously made £1 billion pounds by 'short-selling' pounds. This was the practice of selling securities not yet owned with a view to buying them at a lower price later, a form of sophisticated gambling. It was disastrous for the UK government which estimated the cost to the UK Treasury at £3.4 billion.

The European sovereign-debt crisis is another example which demonstrates clearly the economic weaknesses of nation states. This on-going financial crisis illustrates how difficult it has been for some countries to service their debts without massive support from outside sources. In the early 2000s several states failed to keep internationally agreed debt and deficit targets. From 2009 fears of a sovereign debt crisis as a result of rising private and government debt levels led to a wave of downgrading of government debt in several European states. Among the reasons was the US subprime mortgage crisis of 2007-8 which had a domino effect with negative consequences throughout the global economy, including the EU where the property bubble burst, notably in Ireland and

Spain. In Greece and Cyprus, for example, austerity measures required by the 'Troika' (EU, ECB and IMF) as a condition for bailouts led to serious unrest and the danger of civil strife. Governments had to walk the difficult tightrope between agreeing to these conditions and enraging their civilian populations who felt they had not been responsible for the crisis. Across Europe people have become disillusioned and divided by the debt crisis and support for the EU has seriously declined. In the UK this has been reflected in the rise of support for UKIP. Another consequence in many countries has been the high levels of unemployment, especially among young people. Across the EU nearly one quarter of those aged 15-24 are jobless with the figures being 59% in Greece and 56% in Spain. There are serious fears of 'a lost generation', many of whom are seeking employment abroad.

Apart from the military and economic weaknesses of nation states there are also plenty of examples of political weaknesses. In the US President Obama has had great difficulty promoting welfare or health care reforms in the face of a hostile Republican Congress. Currently in the UK David Cameron is having a torrid time with eurosceptic members of his own party. In all democracies, there is an obvious constraint on the pursuit of long-term developments or reforms where these are likely to have short-term electoral consequences. Examples include the challenges to high-speed rail links and extra airport runways or to a serious national housebuilding programme by NIMBY ('not in my backyard') interests. Governments of various shades have for decades failed to address the need to reform the welfare state and benefits system and pension arrangements in spite of the rapid ageing of the population.

In sum, no nation-state in this globalised and heavily interdependent world of today has absolute power whether militarily, economically, politically or culturally. In many ways the biggest threats today come from inter-ethnic conflicts and various forms of terrorism which necessitate interstate collaboration and response. Similarly, no nation-state is entirely independent economically and must trade internationally in either food and/or materials or energy sources. Politically, in the age of transnational forms of instant communication, even China is beginning to appreciate the need to respond to the demands of its population. In democratic societies these demands are so great that short-termism in decision-making seriously inhibits long-term planning. Finally, no single culture has absolute power. Hollywood is challenged by Bollywood, Christianity by Islam, religion by secularism, neo-liberal capitalism by various forms of community-oriented democracy. Every nation has its weaknesses, limitations and needs and increasingly there is awareness of global problems such as climate change and food and water shortages which necessitate responses of international collaboration.

3. The Drive for International Regulation

(a) The UN and its Various Agencies

Following the First World War the League of Nations was set up to maintain world peace and prevent wars through collective security and disarmament and the settling of international disputes through negotiation and arbitration. At its peak in 1935 it had 58 members. But in the 1930s the Axis powers withdrew and the Great Powers were often reluctant to enforce its resolutions. Ultimately it failed to prevent the Second World War and it was dissolved in 1946. The UN which replaced it inherited a number of agencies and organisations founded by the League.

The UN Charter was formally signed by 50 nations in 1945 after being ratified by the five permanent members of the Security Council. Today 193 countries are members. The Preamble to the Charter sets out its basic aims:

'We the peoples of the United Nations determined: to save succeeding generations from the scourge of war... and to reaffirm faith in fundamental human rights, in the dignity and worth of the human person, in the equal rights of men and women and or nations large and small, and to establish conditions under which justice and respect for the obligations arising from treaties and other sources of international law can be maintained, and to promote social progress and better standards of life in larger freedom...'

It is interesting to note the concern not only to prevent war, mediate conflicts and maintain peace, but also promote human rights and development. Thus among its numerous agencies are the United Nations Economic and Social Council which coordinates the work of such autonomous organisations as the International Labour Organisation (ILO), the Food and Agriculture Organisation (FAO), the United Nations Educational, Scientific and Cultural Organisation (UNESCO), the World Health Organisation (WHO), the World Bank Group, the International Monetary Fund (IMF), the UN Children's Fund (UNICEF), the UN High Commissioner for Refugees (UNHCR), and the UN Development Programme (UNDP).

The international pursuit of the peaceful resolution of conflicts has been a major aim of the UN over the past six decades. While it has not successfully outlawed war it has been instrumental in bringing about the peaceful resolution of conflicts in many parts of the world. There are numerous current examples of its activities. For example, in Africa it is involved in assisting several nations such as Burundi, Kenya, Libya, Mali, Sierra Leone, Sudan and Somalia cope with civil war or long-standing political instability. In Central America UN envoys helped forge peace agreements in El Salvador and Guatemala. In Asia it is providing support in Myanmar as it passes through a transitory phase after years of military rule and in Sri Lanka it has been helping in the dignified return and resettlement of civilians uprooted by years of civil conflict. In Europe it is assisting in the search for a comprehensive and mutually acceptable settlement to the problems in Cyprus and in resolving a dispute between Greece and the former Republic of Macedonia. In the Middle East it is seeking a two-state solution to the Israeli-Palestinian conflict and attempting to mediate in the bloody civil war in Syria. It is working to ensure lasting peace in Lebanon and providing assistance to Iraq's post-war political transition.

In 1948 the Universal Declaration of Human Rights was adopted by the UN General Assembly. It suggested that the inherent dignity and equal and inalienable rights of every human person was the foundation of freedom, justice and peace in the world. It urged that all 'should act towards one another in a spirit of brotherhood'; that 'everyone has the right to life, liberty and security'; that the slave trade should be prohibited; that 'no one shall be subject to torture or to cruel, inhuman or degrading treatment or punishment'; and much more besides. It is obvious that hardly a day goes by without some new evidence of human rights violations including child abuse, sex trafficking, and the rendition and torture of prisoners in secret locations. In 2009 Amnesty International reported that torture or abuse occurred in at least 81 countries, unfair trials in at least 54 countries, and restrictions on freedom of expression in at least 77 countries. Clearly much remains to be achieved but international campaigning groups such as Amnesty International put relentless pressure on those with decision-making power to reform.

The UN Development Programme (UNDP) partners people at all levels of society in 177 countries to help nations withstand crises, such as famine in Africa, and drive and sustain the kind of growth that improves the quality of life for everyone. It links and coordinates global and national efforts to reach the Millennium Development Goals which aim to cut poverty by half by 2015. It encourages the protection of human rights and the empowerment of women. It produces an annual Human Development Report which focuses global debate on key development issues, provides innovative analysis and often controversial policy proposals.

In sum, the UN and its various agencies seek to achieve peace and the resolution of conflicts by means of international collaboration, the promotion of human rights and the empowerment of women, and the social, political and economic development of nations by sustained negotiation and collaboration with all interested parties. In an increasingly interdependent world, collaboration and conciliation between nations are essential for the preservation of peace and the progression of development. There is no doubt that the UN requires serious reform. For example, the Security Council's five veto-wielding permanent members – China, France, Russia, the UK and US – reflect the world of 1945; this needs to be amended to reflect better the realities of the twenty-first century. In an increasingly globalised and interdependent world the UN is an important step on the way to a more collaborative world.

(b) The European Union and Regional Collaboration.

It could be argued that the fear of further military conflict between France and Germany, after three wars in seventy years, was responsible for the setting up of the European Coal and Steel Community by six nations in 1950. This was the beginning of growing cooperation between the states of Western Europe which led in 1957 to the signing of the Treaty of Rome creating the European Economic Community (EEC), expanding economic cooperation, creating a 'common market' and allowing the free movement of people, goods and services across borders, and joint control over food production and the 'Common Agricultural Policy' to ensure that everyone had enough to eat. In 1973 Denmark, Ireland and the UK joined the European Union and the EU Regional Policy began transferring funds to create jobs and infrastructure in poorer areas. Greece joined the EU in 1981 and Spain and Portugal in 1986. In 1986 the Single European

Act was signed creating the 'Single Market'. In 1995 Austria, Finland and Sweden joined and a further ten in 2004 and two in 2007.

In 1999 the Euro was introduced and banknotes and coins entered circulation in 2002. It is the official currency of 17 of the 27 member states of the EU and is the second largest reserve currency and second most traded currency in the world after the US dollar. But the current economic crisis has drawn attention to some serious difficulties which arise when individual states no longer have complete political control over their economic policies. With hindsight, it is apparent that there needs to be a closer relationship between economic and political decision-making. In other words, the logic of the current problems with the Euro is that there needs to be some sort of movement towards a United States of Europe with more centralised economic decision-making and social policy. This is clearly unacceptable to most people in the UK and it would seem also to be the case in many countries across Europe. People want to maintain their national independence even if it is only nominal.

But the advantages of closer collaboration are considerable. The EU is the world's largest single market with around 500 million people. It enables not just free trade in terms of the absence of tariffs but also a common set of rules which means that businesses do not have to comply with 27 different sets of regulations. The European Court of Justice has prevented restrictions of trade and the convergence of employment and welfare arrangements has arguably favoured the interests of workers. For the tourist there are clearly great advantages in there being a single currency. In sum, the European Union is a great example of the advantages of promoting greater collaboration and some sense of common identity between nations which in the past have had a history of serious conflict.

(c) The World Bank and International Monetary Fund

A third example of the imperative to seek international regulation and collaboration in a globalised world is to be found in the major international financial institutions, such as the World Bank and IMF, set up at the Bretton Woods Conference in 1944. The World Bank provides loans to developing countries for capital programmes. Its official goal is the reduction of poverty but many of its policies have been criticised. By tradition its President has always been a US citizen and this again seems to reflect the power differentials of an earlier age.

The IMF describes itself as 'an organisation of 188 countries, working to foster global monetary cooperation, secure financial stability, facilitate international trade, promote high employment and sustainable economic growth, and reduce poverty around the world.' The IMF controversially requires certain conditions to be met before making loans to countries. This may entail various types of structural adjustments such as cutting expenditures (austerity), devaluation of currencies, trade liberalisation and so on. Such policies have often been criticised for being insensitive to local realities, for example in Africa, undermining domestic political institutions. Joseph Stiglitz, a Nobel prize winner and former chief economist at the World Bank has criticised the austerity programmes of the IMF as 'reflecting the interests and ideology of the Western financial community'. One proposed reform is a movement towards closer partnership with other specialised agencies such as UNICEF, the FAO and UNDP.

In sum, both the World Bank and the IMF grew out of the post-war moves to seek greater collaboration in financial matters and assistance for states under temporary difficulties. In a globalising world the need for some sort of regulation and mutual support has become increasingly apparent. With recent developments in communications and information technology, there is a need to control speculative attacks on currency valuations which seriously undermine the decision-making power of independent states. One helpful suggestion is that of a 'Tobin tax' on short-term foreign exchange transactions in order to cushion exchange rate fluctuations. The European Commission in 2011 proposed such a EU financial transaction tax though non-Eurozone countries such as the UK and Sweden unfortunately strongly resisted the proposal.

Generally it can be said that attempts are being made to ensure greater regulation of international financial dealings and to promote the fairness of the development of struggling countries, especially in the southern hemisphere. Inevitably such efforts are resisted by powerful commercial and financial interests, chiefly in the more developed countries in the northern hemisphere. Slowly communitarian efforts are being made to improve the fairness of development processes and generate a growing awareness of the need to share more fairly the finite goods of the increasingly interdependent world in which we live.

4. New Alliances

Many developing countries share a colonial history. As has often been recognised, the ending of political colonialism has frequently been replaced by forms of economic colonialism which maintained the dependence of former colonies on their former colonial masters. Among the countervailing forces resisting the dominance of powerful military, economic, political and cultural forces in our contemporary world is the emergence of a number of international self-help groups. Among these might be listed the BRIC countries, and the D8 and N11 countries in contrast to the G8 developed countries. These new alliances reflect the attempt to provide countervailing forces to the powerful developed countries and the international institutions they control.

As has been mentioned earlier, the BRIC countries (Brazil, Russia, India and China) have the demographic and economic potential to rank among the world's largest and most influential economic powers. Together they comprise more than 2.8 billion people or 40% of the world's population and currently contribute more than 25% of global gross domestic product (GDP). Recently, for example, along with South Africa, they announced the setting up of a business council aimed at strengthening trade and investment between themselves and reducing their reliance on developed countries as the balance of global economic power shifts.

Analysts have also identified the 'Next 11' (N 11) countries as economically dynamic and promising developing countries with the potential to play significant roles in the global economy. Some of these, the D-8 or Developing Eight countries, Bangladesh, Egypt, Indonesia, Iran, Malaysia, Nigeria, Pakistan and Turkey, which have large Muslim populations, have formed an economic development alliance to improve their position in the global economy, diversify and create new opportunities for trade, enhance participation in decision-making at the international level, and improve their standards of living. Pointedly, the first Summit Declaration in 2007 stated that socio-economic development was to be pursued in line with six principles: peace instead of conflict; dialogue instead of confrontation; cooperation instead of exploitation; justice instead of double standards; equality instead of discrimination; and democracy instead of oppression. This agenda reminds us that the perspectives of developing countries have been moulded by their experiences of control by the developed countries in the past and that now they are feeling increasingly strong and aim to flex their muscles in the years to come.

As I write this section, the Africa Union is celebrating fifty years since the signing of the Charter of the Organisation of African Unity (OAU). In 2002 it was replaced by the African Union (AU) of 54 African states; the only African state not a member is Morocco. Among its objectives are to achieve greater unity and solidarity between the African countries; to accelerate the political and socio-economic integration of the continent; to promote and defend African common positions on issues of interest to the continent and its peoples; to establish the necessary conditions which enable the continent to play its rightful role in the global economy and in international negotiations; and to promote sustainable development at the economic, social and cultural levels as well as the integration of African economies. Interestingly it also wished to encourage international cooperation, taking due account of the Charter of the United Nations and the Universal Declaration of Human Rights and stressed the intention of working with relevant international partners in the eradication of preventable diseases and the promotion of good health on the continent.

In sum, there are several examples of the mobilisation of countervailing power by the developing countries and this is likely to become an increasingly important reality in the global relations which develop throughout your lifetimes.

5. The Consequences of Errors of Judgement

Opinions will no doubt continue to be divided by the wars in Iraq and Afghanistan. I am amazed to see that it is already ten years since I joined the huge anti-war demonstration in London. A French academic has estimated that in early 2003 36 million people across the world took part in some 3000 protests against the Iraq war. It is sobering to realise that such large protests in democratic societies were substantially ineffective in persuading political leaders, especially in the US and UK, not to go ahead with their plans to topple Saddam Hussein, the Iraq dictator. I suggest that in the context of this letter it is an important reminder of the relative weakness of countervailing forces to the concentrations of power among the political, economic and military elites. The supposed justification in terms of dangerous concentrations of 'weapons of mass destruction' and the intention to use them against western powers was subsequently shown to be false.

Similar criticisms might be made of the war in Afghanistan supposedly to root out supporters of Al Qaeda. Again, many in the political and military elites would argue that the global Islamist organisation founded by Osama bin Laden in 1988/9 has been seriously damaged by the war in Afghanistan and that the shoots of a democratic state have been well and truly set. But the counter evidence is strong. Afghanistan is basically a tribal society and over the past century and more it has resisted every attempt by outside forces, Britain historically but also Russia most recently, to subdue it. The Taliban, an Islamic fundamentalist political movement in Afghanistan enforced its strict interpretation of Sharia law when it was in power before the American-led invasion in 2001. It has regrouped as an insurgency movement and has been accused of using terrorism as a specific tactic to further its ideological and political goals.

Both these examples point to the dangerous consequences of errors of judgement. There are good grounds for believing that it was a major error of judgement to categorise the response to the terrorist attacks in New York, London, Bali and Madrid as a 'war against terror' which led to attacks on two sovereign states. Rather it could be argued that there should have been efforts to seek international collaboration in the pursuit of terrorists who had committed major crimes in several countries. Instead the two wars have had serious consequences and have led to an increase of anti-west sentiment and a mobilisation of many Muslims to fight against the secularising tendencies they see in the West. Furthermore, according to the United Nations, the Taliban and its allies have been responsible for up to 80% of civilian casualties in Afghanistan.

In sum, the wars in Iraq and Afghanistan are a sober reminder that stable and viable democracies cannot be achieved solely by the imposition of superior military might. We in the West need to learn these lessons as our modern world increasingly reflects the interests of the developing nations and former colonial territories in the southern hemisphere. We need to be more humble and prepared to dialogue without assumptions of continuing superiority. Terrorism can only be satisfactorily addressed by means of international collaboration, not brute force.

6. Conclusion

In the previous letter it was suggested that many of the problems of our contemporary world, both within our own nation and also internationally between nations, reflected the powerful dominance of neo-liberal capitalist institutions, such as banks and multinational commercial giants, and the support given them by political leaders, backed up where it was felt necessary by military power and by the cultural messages given out by the powerful mass media substantially controlled by commercial interests. In other words we live in a fallen, dysfunctional and imperfect world. This letter has endeavoured to be hopeful and find evidence of countervailing forces striving to reform our present world. It suggested that:

- The social reality of our imperfect world of inequality and injustice needs to be challenged and reformed along more communitarian lines which recognise our common human dignity and aim to promote a more sharing and compassionate world by means of dialogue, the peaceful resolution of disputes, and the conciliation of injured parties.

- It was argued that the challenges of war, climate change, food and water shortages and the processes of globalisation require a greater measure of international integration and collaboration and solidarity in pursuit of the global common good.

- It recognised the weaknesses of individual states to achieve complete control over their destinies and hence the need for greater cooperation.
- The drive for international regulation was to be seen in the work of the UN and its many agencies, in the EU, and in the World Bank and IMF.
- New alliances among formerly underdeveloped or colonial countries have emerged in recent years and are likely to provide important countervailing forces to the various institutions of neo-liberal capitalism.
- At the same time we noted the dangers of policy errors by the powerful nations which may hold up the processes of integration.

So, where do we go now? In the second half of this book the focus will be much more on the response of the follower of Jesus, our Lord and saviour. How does His teaching lead us to respond? Part III is entitled 'Christian Analyses' in contrast to the 'Social Analyses' of Part II. In Letter 6 I will suggest we ought to take seriously Jesus' call to seek the Kingdom of God and what that means in terms of basic principles of Catholic social thought as it has developed over the centuries. In Letter 7 we will aim to apply those principles to the main areas of social concern, both domestically and internationally. The final two letters in Part IV will address social action responses to the various issues we have identified.

Part III

Christian Analyses

Letter 6

Seeking The Kingdom

So we come to the third part of our response to the world we are living in, the consideration of Christian analyses of the social reality we outlined in Part I and the social analysis of this reality in terms of structures of injustice and power differentials suggested in Part II. Let us recall that the purpose of my letters to you is to suggest an approach to the matter of how you, as an ordinary Christian, might respond to the call of Jesus to follow Him. I will mainly be referring to Catholic social thought. This is not to neglect or belittle other traditions but to focus on one particular recognised religious framework for our discussions. In this letter I will endeavour to summarise the argument which I have treated at greater length in an earlier book.[5] First, I will address Jesus' call to His followers to seek the Kingdom of God here on earth as in heaven. Secondly, I will suggest that being a Christian citizen means taking seriously the key slogans of the French Revolution of over 200 years ago, viz. liberty, equality and fraternity. Thirdly, I will outline some of the key principles enunciated in Catholic social thought as it has evolved, especially over the past 120 years. Fourthly, I will reflect on

[5] Readers who wish to pursue the topic of this chapter further may like to consult M.P.Hornsby-Smith, *An Introduction to Catholic Social Thought*, Cambridge University Press, 2006, Chapters 3-5.

the calling of the ordinary Christian in today's globalising world.

1. Jesus' Call to Seek the Kingdom of God

In the Sermon on the Mount Jesus urged people to trust in providence, stop worrying about everyday concerns and seek the kingdom of God *first* (Mt. 6: 33). In the Lord's Prayer we pray 'Thy kingdom come, thy will be done, *on earth* as it is in heaven' (Mt. 6:10). Jesus also told us that 'the kingdom of God is amongst you' (Lk. 17:21). Yet before Pilate, Jesus insisted that his kingdom was not of this world (Jn. 18:36). How can these statements be reconciled? Scripture scholars do so in terms of the phrase 'already but not yet'. Jesus inaugurated the kingdom of God which is present in the here and now but it remains to be fully realised at the end of time when Satan's powers of domination and oppression are finally defeated by God's power of service and freedom.

Matthew's Gospel mentions the kingdom of heaven (God) no fewer than fifty-five times and has been described as a dramatic account in seven acts of the coming of the kingdom of heaven: the preparation, first proclamation, preaching by missionaries, obstacles to be expected, embryonic existence among the first disciples, the crisis provoked by the Jewish leaders, and the coming effected through Jesus' Passion and Resurrection. Jesus never defined what He meant by 'the kingdom of God' but presented its meanings in symbolic actions such as table fellowship with all sorts of people, and in the parables which testified to a compassionate God. While the full realisation of God's kingdom was to be in the future, the kingdom had been initiated and was a present reality. We cannot build the kingdom of God; that is God's work. But we are called to be collaborators in seeking it.

There are numerous occasions in the gospels where Jesus stresses the social dimension of His call to proclaim the 'good news to the poor' and oppressed. In his visit to Nazareth he reads the text from Isaiah (61:1-2): 'The spirit of the Lord is on me, for he has anointed me to bring the good news to the afflicted. He has sent me to proclaim liberty to captives, sight to the blind, to let the oppressed go free, to proclaim a year of favour from the Lord' (Lk. 4: 18). It was passages such as this that led liberation theologians in Latin America to develop a critique of the structures of dominance and oppression in today's world. For Gustavo Gutiérrez the elimination of misery and exploitation, oppression, slave like conditions of work, and the evil and scandal of poverty 'will signify the coming of the kingdom.' Jon Sobrino summed up Jesus' mission of fidelity to the Father as proclaiming the kingdom of God and denouncing 'every form of oppression that was practised by the economically strong, the intellectuals, the religious leaders, and the political leaders'.

The teaching authority of the Catholic Church was concerned about the secularist interpretations of the coming of an earthly kingdom of justice arising from some elements of liberation theology and argued for a Christian practice of liberation in accordance with the supreme commandments of love of God and neighbour. Nevertheless, in my view, the approach of liberation theologians fits in well with the theme that Jesus came to proclaim and inaugurate the kingdom of God on earth and that it is the task of his followers to seek this kingdom where God reigns in justice and peace.

One of the characteristics of the kingdom of God is justice, which the *Catechism* tells us is one of the four cardinal virtues. It is defined as 'the moral virtue that consists in the constant and firm will to give their due to God and neighbour... and to establish in human relationships the harmony that promotes equity with regard to persons and to the common good'. The Judeo-Christian understanding of justice looks forward in hope to God's kingdom of justice and love which is in stark contrast to the notion that liberal democracy is the ultimate legitimate hope for the world.

The biblical concept of justice has to do with *right relations* to God, one's neighbour and creation as a whole. The Old Testament interprets this in terms of the ideal Covenant relationships in which 'I will be your God and you will be my people'. Micah (6:8) tells us that Yahweh only wanted the Israelites 'to act justly, love tenderly, and walk humbly with your God.' God treated people not according to their deserts but according to their needs. Hence the special concern for the poor, orphans, widows and foreigners. The Great Jubilee every fifty years required the Israelites to return to their ancestral properties, thus preventing the creation of land monopolies. The Covenant ideal was egalitarian and participative and required the conversion of people to this ideal and the restructuring and transformation of socio-political structures and institutions to realise it. In 1971 the Synod of Bishops famously taught that:

> Action on behalf of justice and participation in the transformation of the world fully appear to us as a constitutive dimension of the preaching of the Gospel, or, in other words, of the Church's mission for the redemption of the human race and its liberation from every oppressive situation.

In other word, justice-seeking is no 'optional extra' but an essential element in Christian discipleship. How this might work out in practice has been addressed by a number of eminent writers such as the philosopher John Rawls who saw justice in terms of fairness, and Amartya Sen whose approach to equality was to focus on individual capabilities. Both authors are well-worth following up.

2. Christian Citizenship

This leads us to explore more secular interpretations and analyses of the concept of citizenship and of such values as freedom, equality and solidarity. How might they be reflected in any realisation of the kingdom of God 'on earth as in heaven'? Some of these values, principles and ideologies which arose in secular society were bitterly resisted for decades by the Catholic Church and have only come to be accepted in recent years. In particular the Second Vatican Council (1962-5) stressed the value of dialogue between Christian perspectives, other faiths and secular ideas. The Catholic concept of citizenship is to be found in seeking the 'Common Good'. Secular concepts of citizenship and its three characteristics of liberty, equality and fraternity (expressed as solidarity in modern papal teaching) emerged out of the French revolution of 1789.

One obvious right of citizenship is that of ***participation*** in key areas of social life. This includes participation in (a) the political life of society, in the election of representatives, decision-makers and civil authorities, and the determination of social policies; (b) in the economic life of society normally through paid employment which provides self-respect and a wage necessary to bring up a family and accumulate property; and (c) in the social and cultural life of society. Participation as a right derives from the notion of the intrinsic dignity of each individual human being who, for Christians, is called to participate in the extension of God's creation through productive work and to contribute to the common good. Participation also implies and is related to the notions of individual freedom, equality and solidarity. From an initial distrust of the power of the state following the French Revolution, papal thinking now insists on 'the *basic right* to participate in the choices of society'.

Let us consider the three great slogans of the French Revolution, firstly, individual ***freedom***. The core teaching on freedom is derived from Jesus' teaching that 'the truth will make you free' (Jn 8: 32). Yet the Catholic Church was extraordinarily slow to recognise the importance of freedom in God's world. The democratic stirrings of the French Revolution were seen as challenges to the monarchical rights of the popes as rulers of the Church and of the papal states. It was not until the final session of the Second Vatican Council in 1965 that the age-old antipathy to religious freedom was laid to rest. But the remaining suspicions among the Vatican authorities were reflected in their concerns about liberation theology. Liberation was seen primarily as 'liberation from the radical slavery of sin', including 'in the cultural, economic, social and political spheres'. Related to this is the ancient tradition that 'error has no rights', leading to inevitable tensions over the rights and limits of individual conscience. The Catholic sense of freedom is radically different from individual licence or uncontrolled economic liberalism because they fail to take into account the dignity of people. Real freedom is the absence from both individual sin and social or structural sin and is a mark of the kingdom of God which has already been revealed to us by Jesus, but which remains to be sought and witnessed to in our everyday lives.

The second of the three great slogans of the French Revolution is ***equality***. The concept of equality is perhaps the least developed and promoted characteristic of the kingdom of God in Catholic social thought. There seems to be a lack of concern positively to promote equality as opposed to the rather unspecific advocacy of reduced inequalities. Yet I would suggest that equality is an essential characteristic of the kingdom of God and therefore a good which followers of Christ should seek and strive for. There has been a long historical tradition that the Church is not a democracy and is intrinsically hierarchical and so unequal. As I write this it is possible that Pope Francis I might be challenging that assumption. Only with the Second Vatican Council did the Church begin the process of valuing the equality of all the People of God which has been advocated in secular thought now for two centuries. Amartya Sen has rightly asked 'equality of what?' since all human beings have different gifts and capacities and he has proposed a focus on an individual's 'capability to achieve functionings that he or she has reason to value'. What is important is to seek social, political and economic conditions which ensure that all persons are treated as moral equals.

All human beings share equally in having been created in the image of God. The Fall showed that inequality was a punishment and subversive of the kind of fellowship God wills for his people. The Old Testament is full of reminders that strangers were to be treated 'as though they were native-born' and the prophets constantly reminded that structures of equality and justice are the clear will of God. In the New Testament there is a great emphasis on the universalistic norm of treating everyone alike. Jesus broke barriers of status and power, for example in table fellowship, and in the parable of the labourers in the vineyard (Mt.20:1-16) the landowner paid all in relation to their equal need. This is a prophetic challenge to us to give serious attention to the notion of equality. The kingdom of God ought to reflect the characteristics of the Trinity: the citizens of the kingdom will be diversely distinct, equal and have parity of esteem in the sight of God, and relate to each other in fraternal love and solidarity.

The third of the slogans of the French Revolution was fraternity which might roughly be translated as ***solidarity***. This has been much stressed in recent Catholic social teaching. The Second Vatican Council talked about a needful solidarity where everyone 'would render mutual service according to the different gifts bestowed on each.' For the Polish Pope John Paul II worker solidarity was a 'just social reaction' to unjust working conditions and exploitation. Paul VI argued that 'there can be no progress toward the complete development of man without the simultaneous development of all humanity in the spirit of solidarity.' We are all together in this one world which we are called to share. This imposes a moral duty on both individuals and nations to face up to our responsibilities to share the goods of this earth.

Pope John Paul II suggested that there was a 'growing awareness of interdependence among individuals and nations'. For him the virtue of solidarity was 'a firm and persevering determination to commit oneself to the common good.' Peace was the fruit of solidarity which 'seeks to go beyond itself, to take on the specifically Christian dimension of total gratuity, forgiveness and reconciliation'. With solidarity our neighbour 'becomes the living image of God the Father, redeemed by the blood of Jesus Christ and placed under the permanent action of the Holy Spirit.'

In sum, the concept of solidarity, with its suggestive secular roots in French revolutionary history and worker movements for social justice, has been elaborated in much recent social thought as an awareness of the interdependence of peoples has become more apparent under globalisation. But it also has important biblical roots which have been articulated, notably by recent popes, in contemporary Catholic social thought.

In this section I have suggested that there are important signposts towards the kingdom of God to be found in the French Revolution's slogans of liberty, equality and fraternity in a society characterised by democratic participation. Each of these characteristics has deep scriptural roots, even if for long periods of history they were forgotten or resisted. Today they are among the defining principles of Catholic social thought.

3. Catholic Social Thought: Basic Principles

Teaching nearly 2000 years ago Jesus did not tell us how to cope with the injustices of international debt or the global recession, or about nuclear, chemical, biological or cyber warfare, or about genetic engineering or how to tackle the problems of social exclusion or climate change. In this section I will offer an overview of how Catholic social thought has developed, especially over the past 120 years or so, in its attempt to respond to these issues as Jesus would have wanted us to do.

One of the first things to note about Catholic social thought is that it is not static but dynamic in response to changing circumstances and needs. Indeed, on certain matters, such as slavery, democracy, human rights and religious freedom, earlier positions have been reversed. Secondly, for the past 120 years or so it has sought to articulate a path between communism or state socialism and liberal capitalism and has insisted that the purpose of the economy is to serve the needs of people. Thirdly, two different approaches have been used in the development of Catholic social thought: scripture and the appeal to revelation, and natural law thinking in principle accessible to all people of good will. The relative emphasis between these two approaches has changed over the years. Fourthly, Catholic social thinking flows from a wide range of sources including the teaching of the Second Vatican Council; papal encyclicals perhaps best regarded as articulating the 'mind of the Church' as it has evolved over time in ever-changing social, cultural, economic and political contexts; collegial teaching such as those emerging from Synods or Bishop's Conferences; the insights of liberation or feminist theologians; the insights of those in the burgeoning number of non-governmental organisations and campaigning groups; or academic theologians, philosophers and social scientists producing critical analyses and evaluations of Catholic social thought.

As we journey through the first quarter of the twenty-first century it might be helpful to reflect on six key concepts or guiding principles of Catholic social thought. While there is general agreement about these principles it is recognised that 'they still need a lot of working through and connecting by way of middle-level thinking, to ideas for policy'. Perhaps you might be inspired to contribute to this in a world which is changing so fast.

The first concept, ***human dignity***, 'the inviolable dignity of every human person', is regarded as 'the basis of official

Catholic social teaching' which is 'a transcendent value, always recognised as such by those who sincerely search for the truth'. This suggests a natural law claim until it is expressed in terms of the story of creation and the revelation that every human person has been 'created by God in His image and likeness as well as redeemed by the most precious blood of Christ... called to be... a living temple of the Spirit, destined for the eternal life of blessed communion with God'. In his encyclical letter, *Pacem in Terris* (Peace on Earth) in 1963 Pope John XXIII had constructed an argument for the recognition of human rights on the basis of 'the dignity of the human person in the light of divinely revealed truth'.

The second concept is that of the ***common good*** which recognizes the interdependence of human beings and 'rejects the individualistic presuppositions of that form of liberal thought rooted in the Enlightenment notion of human autonomy'. The Second Vatican Council suggested that the common good referred to 'the sum total of social conditions which allow people, either as groups or as individuals, to reach their fulfilment more fully and more easily'. It presupposed respect for individual people and social groups and their access to what was necessary to lead a fully human life, and a stable, secure and just social order. This requires a form of conversion which would affect attitudes and behaviour towards neighbours, human communities such as ethnic minorities, refugees or migrant workers, animals and the whole natural world, all of which are involved in the common good. The bishops of England and Wales famously wrote in 1996: 'that common good is the whole network of social conditions which enable human individuals and groups to flourish and live a fully, genuinely human life, otherwise described as "integral human development". All are responsible for all, collectively, at the level of society or nation, not only as individuals'.

It is interesting that in different ways and somewhat indirectly both the main political parties have in recent years proposed slogans which have some relationship to the notion of the common good. David Cameron and the coalition government refer to the 'big society', though the underlying motive and intention might well be the 'small state'! Meanwhile Labour talks about 'one nation', but this might well be more rhetoric than practical policies.

The third principle, ***subsidiarity***, emerged in a papal encyclical in 1931 and reflects the Church's long-standing fear of state control. In response it teaches that 'a community of a higher order should not interfere in the internal life of a community of a lower order, depriving the latter of its functions, but rather should support it in case of need and help co-ordinate its activity with the activities of the rest of society, always with a view to the common good'. It defends the right to associate and organise and the rights of individuals and families in their relationships with the state. It encouraged the establishment of a healthy plurality of intermediate associations such as trade unions. In our time the principle has relevance for the relationship between central government and the local authorities. It has been appealed to by nations in their relationships with the European Union and within the Church to the rights of bishops' conferences in their relationships with the Vatican Curia.

The fourth principle is ***the preferential option for the poor*** which emerged out of liberation theology in Latin America in the 1960s. As has been mentioned previously, liberation theology was regarded with suspicion by the Vatican authorities because of some Marxist influences in it. This 'counter-offensive' against the concept is, perhaps, reflected in Pope John Paul II's tortuous reference to 'the preferential option or love of preference for the poor... a special form of primacy in the exercise of Christian charity.' The notion, which is solidly rooted in both the Old and New Testaments, commits Christians to resist 'the injustice, oppression, exploitation and marginalization of people that permeate almost every aspect of public life... (and) to disengage from serving the interests of the powerful and instead to take the side of those who are relatively powerless'.

The fifth principle is that of ***solidarity*** was mentioned above in the discussion of the French revolutionary concept of 'fraternité'. In reaction to liberal capitalism and extreme individualism it stresses our common humanity and responsibility for others. It relates not just to workers within societies but also to relationships between developed and developing nations in a globalising world. It was strongly emphasised by Pope John Paul II for whom solidarity 'is not a feeling of vague compassion... at the misfortunes of so many people, ...(but) a firm and persevering determination to commit oneself to the common good'. It is suggested that its significance in Catholic social thought goes beyond enlightened self-interest 'to signify an attitude which finds its image in the common fatherhood of God and the brotherhood of all in Christ – a solidarity which finds its concrete expression in bearing radical witness to the love of our neighbour, so that it makes us ready for sacrifice'. It has been argued that solidarity is open in the direction of love, and is the lead value for all the other interdependent values. Catholic beliefs in the Trinity's diverse distinctiveness, absolute equality and perfect love foster 'a desire for diversity, parity and love to be combined *even* in the temporal world'. Finally, it has been argued that 'the constellation and inter-penetration of concepts (in Catholic social thought) is distinct: of human dignity, solidarity, subsidiarity, social justice, the option for the poor, the common good, justice as participation, etc'.

It has been suggested that an emerging sixth principle in Catholic social thought is that of a ***preferential option for non-violence***. It is clearly implicit in recent Catholic thought about war and peace. As we shall see in the next letter, the traditional conditions for a 'just war' increasingly fail to be met in modern, technologically sophisticated warfare where the evidence is of a rapidly increasing proportion of non-combatant deaths. This was reflected in the Second Vatican Council's explicit condemnation of 'total warfare'. In just war thinking war has traditionally been seen as a response of last resort after all attempts at reconciliation have failed. Given the indiscriminate destructive power of modern weapons a preferential option for non-violence clearly ought to be regarded as a basic principle of Catholic social thought.

4. *An Evaluation of Catholic Social Thought*

These six principles together with those of Christian citizenship discussed earlier do not exhaust the riches and resources of Catholic social thought. But they do provide a basic starting point for our reflections on specific policy areas and contributions to 'middle-range' thinking in the following letter. Donal Dorr has helpfully suggested that between 1891 (when Pope Leo XIII wrote the encyclical letter *Rerum Novarum*) and 1961 (when Pope John XXIII wrote *Mater et Magistra*) Catholic Social Doctrine developed a coherent body of teaching around two basic themes:

- a particular concern for the poor and the powerless, together with a criticism of the systems that leave them vulnerable, and
- a defence of certain personal rights, above all the right to private property, against collectivist tendencies.

Dorr suggested that throughout this period the popes were consistently critical of both liberal capitalism and socialism. They also 'put forward certain *fundamental principles* about human nature and the nature of human society in its economic, political, social, cultural and religious aspects', including:

- the right of the individual to own property;
- the right of workers to join trade unions;

- the right of the head of a family to be paid a family wage;
- the duty of governments to work for the common good;
- the right of citizens to resist oppression by lawful means;
- the obligation of governments and the rich and powerful to help the poor;
- the duty of governments and larger agencies to respect the principle of subsidiarity.

Dorr argued that since 1961 there has been 'a decisive move away from the right' and a change in the 'Catholic ethos' alongside the poor in the struggle for justice. Among the *strengths* he identified in Catholic social teaching were:

- it is pluralistic and appealing to all people of good will;
- it focuses on two key humanistic values: participation and solidarity;
- it is based on much social analysis, i.e. it is 'grounded' in social reality;
- it has a strong scriptural basis and it is prophetic 'in the sense of being radically challenging and inspirational'.

Several observers have pointed to a number of *weaknesses* in Catholic social thought:

- it remains somewhat ethnocentric and western, had a limited model of development and was insufficiently ecological;
- it failed to offer an adequate analysis of the root causes of injustice or address the issue of the *social* power of major institutions;
- it paid too little attention to productivity as a social good;
- it assumed social harmony, embraced the *status quo* and failed to suggest alternatives and overlooked pluralism.

- it failed to offer positive advocacy of equality or of non-violence;
- it has failed to dialogue convincingly with secular thought and analyses.
- it neglected women.

For Catholics justice is one of the four 'cardinal' moral virtues that 'consists in the constant and firm will to give their due to God and neighbour'. This is not the same as 'fairness', as perhaps the parable of the workers in the vineyard (Mt. 20: 1-16) makes clear and where need is the determining factor. The Catholic interpretation of justice sees itself as part of an evolving and refining Judeo-Christian ethic. The teachings of Jesus are indicative, such as the injunction not to take 'an eye for an eye' (Ex 21:24) but to 'turn the other cheek' (Mt 5:39). While the Old Testament prophets and notions of jubilees and sabbaticals (Lev 25:10) are still important, the primacy of the new law to love is emphatic, as in the parable of the Good Samaritan (Lk 10: 29-37). A key text is the account of the last judgement in Matthew's gospel (Mt 25: 31-46) where eternal life or damnation are decided in terms of the extent to which the individual has fed the hungry, given drink to the thirsty, welcomed strangers, clothed the naked, and visited the sick or imprisoned.

Following the Second Vatican Council's Pastoral Constitution on the Church in the Modern World there emerged a strong theme of liberation from sin. That includes the social sin of slavery to oppressive and unjust socio-economic systems. For the first time there are references to 'sinful social structures' and 'a *structural* conflict between the oppressor and the oppressed, between the rich and the poor'. Thus the call to justice includes giving a 'preferential option for the poor', mindful of the preaching of Jesus at Nazareth to 'go and preach the good news to the poor' (Lk 4:18; Is 61:1-2). Strong criticisms of the structural injustices of the dominant forms of liberal capitalism, consumerism and excessive individualism have been articulated in the recent encyclicals of Pope Benedict XVI in *Caritas in Veritate* (2009) and Pope Francis I in *Evangelii Gaudium* (2013).

In sum, justice is seen in right relationships with God and neighbour, and a recognition that all of us are dependent on God for the gifts of this life so that no one can claim absolute property rights over the goods of the earth. Even so, there is still a struggle to realize this in practice and even to convince Church members that the pursuit of justice lies at the heart of what it means to be a Christian and follower of Jesus today.

5. The Call of the Lay Person

In this letter we have begun the task of exploring how best the ordinary Christian might respond to Jesus' call to follow Him in the globalising context of the first quarter of the twenty-first century. What signposts are there for us to follow? We have suggested that a helpful starting point is Jesus' call that we trust in providence, stop worrying about everyday concerns and seek the kingdom of God *first* (Mt 6:33). As He taught us in the Lord's Prayer we are urged to seek the kingdom of God 'on earth as in heaven' (Mt 6:10). We proceeded to explore what it might mean to be a citizen of the kingdom of God and suggested that the secular insights of the French revolution, viz. democratic participation and liberty, equality and fraternity/solidarity, were valuable concepts which have increasingly been recognised by the Catholic Church. We then considered six key principles of modern Catholic social thought: human dignity, the common good, solidarity, subsidiarity, the preferential option for the poor, and the preferential option of non-violence.

All of these concepts have been elaborated in Catholic social thought and especially in recent papal encyclicals. At one point you might want to explore them further but for now, in our globalising world, they are useful starting points for asking yourself 'how should I respond to the various realities and injustices which were outlined in the previous letters' In Letters 2 and 3 we outlined structures of injustice and inequality both internationally, in the relationships between developed and powerful nations and developing and powerless nations in the globalising world, and also comparable inequalities and injustices within our own society. The first stage of our response in Letter 4 was to analyse the inequalities and injustices in our world in terms of differential power relationships, between nations, corporations and individuals. So what do we do in the light of these analyses? Letter 5 made a start by exploring the possibilities of countervailing powers such as prophetic individuals; non-governmental organisations and campaigning groups and their use of modern media communications to raise awareness of social issues very rapidly; and the development of international collaborative efforts to reform major institutions such as the IMF and World Bank and tax laws to ensure large corporations pay their fair share of tax revenues. All these efforts build on a growing consciousness that we live in an interdependent world where collaboration is necessary in the pursuit of the common good. In this letter we began to ask what resources and perspectives can a faith in Christ bring to bear so that we can discern what appropriate response we ought to make to the challenges of our world. In particular we focused on Jesus' call to seek the kingdom of God and encourage its realisation in the world we live in.

The range of problems you will face in your world is truly enormous but it is useful to have at least a basic grasp of what Catholic social thought has to say about some of the more important issues. This will be the task of the following letter where we aim to apply the principles identified in this letter to seven matters of concern both in our own society and in the relationships between nations in our globalising world.

Chapter 7

Critical Perspectives

In the previous letter we considered a range of concepts and principles which have emerged in the development of Catholic social thought particularly over the past 120 years. Our aim in this letter is to apply these general principles to seven significant issues which concern people in the first quarter of the twenty-first century. Hopefully you might be interested in at least one of these areas and will be encouraged and persuaded to follow up your concerns. In this letter I will try to summarise the arguments which I have treated at length in an earlier book.[6]

1. Human rights

The first main area of need and justice is that of human rights in its broadest sense. What do we mean by human rights? Claims range widely and include women's absolute rights over their embryos, parents' claim to choose the gender of their children, gay couples demand for the right to marry and adopt children, the right to privacy and to a good night's sleep under the flight path to a nearby airport, the rights of women and ethnic minorities to equal treatment at work, children's

---

6 Readers who wish to pursue the matters raised in this chapter further may like to consult M.P.Hornsby-Smith, *An Introduction to Catholic Social Thought*, Cambridge University Press, 2006, Chapters 6-11,

right not to be smacked, the right to paid employment, and to choose the time of death. The founding fathers of the US saw the right to life, liberty and the pursuit of happiness as inalienable. The list of claims is endless. A useful starting point comes from recent thinking in Europe which has distinguished several different generations of human rights thinking:

- first generation: civil and political rights, such as the right to life, the prohibition of torture and slavery, freedom of religion, expression, and association;
- second generation: economic and social rights, such as the right to work, social security, protection of the family, necessary for the development of the human person;
- third generation: rights to solidarity, to a healthy environment and to development;
- fourth generation: rights to safeguard human dignity from abuses of technology and biomedicine; and most recently
- fifth generation: of rights to freedom of scientific research and enterprise, protection of intellectual property, to proper administration, children's rights, access to utilities, protection in the event of unfair dismissal, to individual equality before the law and between men and women.

The range of human rights claims is so great that it is no surprise that many are somewhat controversial and clash with other values.

The UN Universal Declaration on Human Rights recognizes the equal dignity and rights of all people and their right to life, liberty, personal security and not to be tortured. With the right to life comes opposition to the death penalty yet nearly eighty nations still retain it. Jesus authoritatively replaced the Old Testament law of retaliation, of 'an eye for an eye', with the ethic of forgiveness (Mt 6:14-15) and the radical challenge to love enemies.

The right to legal justice includes a system of justice which is fair and impartial and treats all brought before the courts as having equal human dignity. Punishments for wrongdoing must be appropriate while respecting the dignity of the prisoner. Given freedom of conscience and the right to dissent which follows from the intrinsic dignity of each human being created in the image of God, there must be concern about the imprisonment of prisoners of conscience. For the same reason the use of torture as an instrument of policy and the corrupt use of rendition must be strongly opposed. In the same way there can be no place for institutions of slavery such as human trafficking.

As I write this, attention has been drawn to the plight of millions of refugees or internally displaced people who are escaping from the ravages and dislocations of war and persecution in their homeland, political dissidents threatened by totalitarian, authoritarian or oppressive regimes who seek asylum elsewhere, and seasonal or long-stay migrant workers who may be escaping from famine or starvation and so have left their homeland in pursuit of work in order to support their families. The Old Testament was absolutely clear on the rights of 'strangers' as well as widows and orphans. In the parable of the last judgement the king will recall: 'I was a stranger and you made me welcome' (Mt 25:35) and invite those who did so into his kingdom. At the creation God instructed us 'to fill the earth and subdue it' (Gen.1:28) and the Catholic Church upholds the right to migrate. We must hear the cries of those subject to discrimination and oppression either as a cause of their migration or as a consequence of it.

Let us consider next the rights of three categories of weak and vulnerable people: ethnic minorities, women and children. In Britain the roots of racism lie deep in our imperial and colonial past and our assumptions of superiority over formerly subject peoples. Racism is the categorization of social groups on the basis of their physical or cultural characteristics as different or inferior. It involves the use of economic, social or political power to justify discrimination, exploitation, and exclusion of a minority group. New Testament teaching stresses 'the unity of humankind'. Christians are called to recognize 'the Gospel of reconciliation' and anticipate the Kingdom of God.

There has been a long history of women's subordination, oppression, exploitation, marginalisation, presumed inferiority, spousal abuse, marital rape and wife-beating, the practice of genital mutilation, restrictions to education and a wide range of systematic institutional discrimination which are all forms of structural sin. Jesus challenged traditional Jewish boundaries as his discussions with the Samaritan woman at the well (Jn 4: 7-26) and the Syro-Phoenician woman (Mk 7:24-30) demonstrated. He had especially close relationships with Martha and Mary and it was to a woman that He first revealed himself after his resurrection (Jn 20:11-18). Justice for women is one area where the Church has failed to respond adequately to secular insights.

Similarly, it is also only in recent decades that we have become sensitized to the violence, oppression, appalling sexual abuses, and injustices perpetrated against children. The area of children's rights in Catholic social thought also needs substantial development.

There is a traditional Catholic insistence that rights are not absolute but must be chosen in accordance with 'natural law'. It rejects the liberal model of the completely sovereign individual but in recognising the intrinsic worth of each individual human being, created in the image of God, it also stresses their responsibility to seek truth and the common good. Yet for all its ambiguities it can be argued that the concept of human rights represents the best chance of affirming the inherent worth and dignity of each and every human being.

As this section on human rights was being drafted there was much concern about the revelation that the secret services in both the US and UK were systematically gaining access to huge amounts of phone and internet data raising serious questions about privacy in the internet age. It is perhaps too soon to make a definitive judgement on the competing rights of the state to national security and the rights of its citizens to individual privacy. But it does seem likely that it is a major issue which you and your generation will have to address.

2. The Family and Related Issues

The Church has traditionally put a great deal of stress on the state's duty to protect 'the family'. But what is the family these days? It has certainly changed quite dramatically in recent decades as a result of technological advances in domestic equipment which have revolutionised domestic work, the availability of the contraceptive pill which has given women greater autonomy over child-bearing, the feminist revolution which has begun to reverse the systematic subordination of women to male domination, increasing levels of divorce so that nearly one half of all marriages end in divorce, declining levels of marriage and increasing levels of cohabitation, high levels of legal abortion, the decriminalisation of homosexuality, and the legalisation of gay marriages and rights to adopt. There is a growing awareness of both physical and sexual abuse within the family. Increasing numbers of children in schools are from 'broken' or reconstituted homes. 'The family' is clearly a more complex phenomenon than a few decades ago. Yet there is general agreement that parenting is an increasingly vital task in a modern and complex society. Social changes and increasing mobility have often diluted three-generational extended families and the support they gave.

In related areas there have also been dramatic changes as a result of biological and technical developments in recent years. More children are being born as a result of IVF (in vitro fertilization). Organ transplants and surgical procedures have contributed to the rapid increase of average life expectancy. There are growing demands for the legalisation of voluntary euthanasia. Developments in genetic engineering are opening up possibilities of cloning and stem cell research and 'manufacturing children' according to taste. The rights of the embryo are coming under increasing threat.

The Church has struggled to keep up with these various developments. The Second Vatican Council (1962-5) referred to the family as 'the first and vital cell of society' and 'the domestic Church'. Yet it offered no serious treatment of the causes of marriage breakdown in the numerous circumstances of stress in the modern world. While it by-passed the issue of contraception it did offer a significant shift in the Church's teaching on marriage and sexuality. In particular, the ancient distinction between the 'primary' end of marriage as procreation and the 'secondary' end the 'avoidance of concupiscence' was ended and due recognition was given to the contribution of sexual intercourse to the development of the human relationship and love between the spouses.

Recent Catholic teaching insists that marriage and family life were willed by God when He created man and woman in His own image and instructed them to be fruitful, multiply and fill the earth. This requires a life-time commitment to parenting, the raising and education of children. Fornication, cohabitation, adultery and divorce are forbidden in the interests of the common good. Procreation should be the result of sexual intercourse between a male and a female and is a participation in the creative power of God. Any interference with the 'natural' course of sexual intercourse, such as IVF, is improper. The 'personalist' aim of sexual intercourse between spouses is a gift of mutual self-giving which contributes to the strengthening of the relationship between them. The Church recognizes the sacramental nature of marriage as a sign of love. Like God's love, then, marriage is indissoluble. The pains and sufferings of married life are interpreted as a participation in the saving work of redemption and in the knowledge that after the cross came the resurrection.

Having children is seen as 'the continuation of creation'. Parents are the 'first and most important educators of their own children' and this needed to be recognised by the State through the family according to the principle of subsidiarity. Families have a right to a decent standard of living and to decent housing and workers have a right to a 'family wage'. Unemployment is seen as 'one of the most serious threats to family life'. Challenges from 'the culture of death' must be tackled by a 'conception of human rights that are developed through the family'. The encyclical *Humanae Vitae* (Paul VI, 1968) reaffirmed the Church's 'constant doctrine... that each and every marriage act must remain open to the transmission of life' though perhaps a large majority of Catholics in the UK and US reject this teaching. Homosexual acts have been interpreted as 'contrary to the natural law' and 'intrinsically disordered' and again, increasing numbers of Catholics contest this.

It is not possible to give a full account here of the Church's position on a range of related issues. For example, patriarchy, that is highly structured forms of gendered inequalities and notions of God-given differences that continue to justify male dominance, continue to be systemic, perhaps especially in the Church. On organ transplants and surgical procedures enhancing life the Church insists on the human dignity of both the donor and the recipient as subjects equal in dignity and value in the sight of God. On abortion and related procedures the traditional Catholic view is that 'life begins at conception'. Euthanasia is regarded as 'morally unacceptable' and palliative care is encouraged. The science of human genetics is advancing at an incredibly rapid rate.

All the issues raised in this section pose challenges which demand urgent attention, proper social and theological analysis and appropriate action in seeking Kingdom values. It is widely recognised that Catholic social teaching in these areas requires some development and the recent survey of experiences and views on marital and family issues is a welcome sign of the recognition of the importance of a lay voice on matters which intimately concern them. In particular it has been suggested that the Church needs to show humility and a readiness to dialogue with biological scientists in a 'continuing conversation'. It also requires a recognition of the compassion of Christ in the case of people in the present world struggling to cope with the wide range of uncertainties in their everyday lives which cannot simply be addressed by following a rule book.

But you, dear reader, in your own family and social relationships are called to recognize the dignity of each and every human being as created in the image of God and behave accordingly.

3. Economic Life

Among the many concerns which you will face throughout your lives will be those of survival and security, of finding a job and earning a wage or salary sufficient to keep you and your family in comfortable accommodation and give them a reasonable standard of living. I am writing this section in the middle of the longest recession for a century. In some countries in Europe at the moment over one half of your age group cannot find work and there are real fears that yours will be a 'lost generation'. You live in a world where substantially deregulated liberal capitalism is dominant, as I discussed above in Letter 4. Short-term profit is often the main driving force. The consequences include job uncertainties, redundancies and unemployment and also widening inequalities. Advocates often assert that 'there is no alternative' to their policies and the increasing power of major banks and corporations. Modern Catholic social thought would contest this and argue for a more regulated and socially conscious economic system as Popes Benedict and Francis have both done in their recent encyclicals.

Numerous problems need to be addressed. High levels of unemployment and the widening gap in incomes and wealth between rich and poor, both domestically and between nations, are matters of concern for social justice and cohesion. Other matters include the protection of worker rights to just wages and pensions, essential for the maintenance of human dignity and the interests of the common good. It is necessary to take account of the impact of demographic changes such as the declining birth rates, increasing life expectancies and ageing of the population, and the changing nature of work due to recent technological developments and IT, and the shift from manufacturing to service sector employment. There needs to be a proper balance between the rights of private property and the common good. Corporate capital has acquired enormous power and there is a need for effective regulation, for example to ensure that they pay fair taxes. The rights of workers to combine in trade unions must be reasserted. There is also a need for the reform of international institutions set up to safeguard the rights of poor countries and ensure just returns for farmers and workers in liberal capitalist economies. This is quite an agenda for action.

What contribution to seeking a just response to these issues has Catholic social thought made? The search for a social and economic system that ensures both political liberty and a reasonable measure of economic equality consistent with the common good is an on-going challenge to the Christian conscience. Over the years there have been significant developments such as the condemnation of slavery and more subtle interpretations of usurious interest rates. Modern Catholic social teaching has traditionally been dated from Pope Leo XIII's encyclical *Rerum Novarum* (1891) which asserted the rights to private property, to a fair wage, and to trade unions. Forty years later Pius XI modified the earlier hostile judgement of communism with a grudging toleration of a 'mitigated socialism' and an insistence on the concept of subsidiarity to counter increasing state power. In *Mater et Magistra* (1961) Pope John XXIII accepted the greater intervention of the state in education and health and expressed a concern for solidarity with future generations, a foretaste, perhaps, of the global ecological concerns which emerged later in the twentieth century.

The Second Vatican Council (1962-5) marked a distinct turning point in the relationship between the Church and the secular world. Its Pastoral Constitution *Gaudium et Spes* (1965) aimed to dialogue about contemporary concerns such as socio-economic life. It again expressed concern about huge economic inequalities and insisted that economic development should be at the service of humankind and that workers were more than 'mere tools of production'. The Latin American bishops at Medellin in 1968 for the first time articulated 'the preferential option for the poor' and in *Octogesima Adveniens* (1971) Paul VI expressed concern at the global process of urbanisation as millions of poor farmers left for the big cities in search of a better life. He also asserted women's equal rights and dignity consistent with her 'proper role... at the heart of the family'. He pleaded for the new poor and marginalised, such as migrant workers, and for those subject to racial discrimination.

Pope John-Paul II made several important contributions to the development of Catholic social thought. *Laborem Exercens* (1981) was noticeable for its shift away from a natural law approach and its strong grounding in scripture, especially the Genesis account of the creation of the human person in the image of God and the vocation to subdue the earth. A consistent concern of the Church's teaching was in making life, including work, more human. He insisted on the ethical nature of work and the dignity of the person doing the work. He reasserted 'the principle of the priority of labour over capital'. The right to private ownership of property was upheld but it was 'subordinated to the right to common use, to the fact that goods are meant for everyone'. Unemployment was always 'an evil' and 'can become a real social disaster', particularly for the young. 'Man, created in the image of God, shares by his work in the activity of the creator'. In *Sollicitudo Rei Socialis* (1987) he stressed that private property 'has an intrinsically social function, based upon and justified precisely by the principle of the universal destination of goods'.

In *Centessimus Annus* (1991) he noted three distinct stages in the emergence of property over the century since *Rerum Novarum*, as land, then capital, and now 'the possession of know-how, technology and skill'. He again drew attention to the 'human inadequacies of capitalism and the resulting domination of things over people'. While the 'free market is the most efficient instrument for utilising resources and effectively responding to needs... the market must be appropriately controlled by the forces of society and by the state to guarantee that the basic needs of the whole of society are satisfied'. The pope warned against the culture of consumerism and 'the risk of an "idolatry" of the market' and 'the loss of the authentic meaning of life' as in consumerism 'when people are ensnared in a web of false and superficial gratifications'.

In 2009 Pope Benedict XVI wrote *Caritas in Veritate* shortly after the credit crisis and the beginning of the global recession which now seems likely to continue until the end of the current decade. There were some important developments in his teaching on economic matters and his reflections on the theme of 'integral human development' which cannot ignore future generations; there is a need for solidarity and inter-generational justice. He is highly critical of speculative financial dealing, the unregulated exploitation of resources, the scandals of glaring inequalities and rigid intellectual property claims. There is a need to tackle the emphasis on 'short-term profit without regard for long-term sustainability' and the structural causes of injustice and 'cultivate a public conscience that considers food and access to water as universal rights of all... without discrimination'. He calls for 'a sustained commitment... to promote a person-based and community-oriented cultural process of world-wide integration that is open to transcendence'. In a clear reference to the causes of the current economic crisis he urges that 'financiers must rediscover the genuinely ethical foundation of their activity..., regulation of the financial sector to safeguard weaker parties and discourage scandalous speculation and experimentation with new forms of finance'. There is a need to construct a social order that at last conforms to the moral order. 'Development is impossible without upright men and women, without financiers and politicians whose consciences are finely attuned to the requirements of the common good'.

Pope Francis I's apostolic exhortation *Evangelii Gaudium* (2013) has some strong criticisms to make about the current economic system. He rejects an economy of exclusion and inequality which kills. 'Today everything comes under the laws of competition and the survival of the fittest, where the powerful feed upon the powerless. As a consequence, masses of people find themselves excluded and marginalised: without work, without possibilities, without any means of escape.' Human beings are treated as consumer goods in a 'throw away' culture. Trickle down free market theories have not been confirmed by the facts and there is a selfish 'globalisation of indifference' towards the excluded and marginalised. The 'idolatry of money' must be rejected. The gap between the rich minority and the majority is growing, defended by 'ideologies which defend the absolute autonomy of the market place and financial speculation.' He rejects a 'deified market' and 'financial system which rules rather than serves' and exhorts us 'to generous solidarity and to a return of economics and finance to an ethical approach which favours human beings'. He rejects 'the inequality which spawns violence', the damage done by 'unbridled consumerism', and the practice of 'blaming the poor'

There is so much in this recent teaching to ponder. I hope it will guide you in your own response to the socio-economic issues which you will inevitably face in your everyday lives.

4. Social Exclusion

Another issue which I suggest should be of concern to the follower of Jesus is that of the social exclusion of some people from full participation in the life of society and from full and effective rights of citizenship in the civil, political and social spheres. A whole range of prejudices such as racism, sexism, homophobia, or towards the young, elderly or disabled, can operate as mechanisms of exclusion, even in the case of those who have adequate material resources. In this sense the concept of social exclusion alerts us to forms of marginalisation in addition to poverty. It can include both absolute and relative forms of poverty or exclusion from adequate income or resources, labour market exclusion from paid employment, service exclusion from education, health and welfare, and exclusion from social relationships including full participation in political processes and decision-making.

The issue of distributive justice within society is undoubtedly controversial. It is suggested than a Christian vision of the dignity of each individual human person, the need to promote the common good of all God's people and solidarity between them, the recognition of the principle of subsidiarity which ensures that social policies properly respect the rights and competencies of individuals, families and local communities, and the obligation to take particular account of the needs of the poor, disadvantaged, weak, disabled and marginalised in society, is essential for the full flourishing and development of the potential of all people in society. Christians should avoid using slogans such as 'skivers' and 'shirkers' which are often generalised to slander large groups of excluded people.

The extent of social inequalities in Britain should be challenging to all Christians. In recent decades the gap between the rich and the poor in terms of both incomes and wealth has steadily widened. Cuts in benefits for the poor while the rich often use sophisticated strategies to avoid paying tax reinforce the trend. As I write child absolute poverty rates are projected to rise from 19% (2.5 millions) in 2010 to 27% (3.9 million) by 2020. There are 2½ million unemployed in Britain and across Europe one quarter of young people are out of work. Millions of those who are in work are on minimum wage levels and more than one half of benefit claimants are in employment. Children from disadvantaged backgrounds have much poorer education achievements. People from disadvantaged backgrounds also have poorer health. There are significant differences both in experiences of crime, such as burglary, and punishment of offenders according to level of disadvantage. Levels of homelessness continue to rise yet levels of building of affordable homes are critically low. Poor people are much more likely to get into debt and be prey to loan sharks, some of whose interest rates have been as high as 5000%. Some ethnic communities suffer from persistent disadvantage and discrimination. Deepening inequality marginalises and excludes the poor from a full social life.

These are some of the characteristics of the society you live in. It will be up to your generation to seek to reverse recent trends and seek a fairer society with lower levels of exclusion and a greater concern for the common good. The ethical case for greater equality, or at least lesser inequality, is that present economic and social structures of inequality inhibit the achievement of that equality of dignity and full participation in society, legally, politically and socially.

Catholic social teaching has struggled to address the issue of equality. Pius XI in 1931 taught that 'the vast differences between the few who hold excessive wealth and the many who live in destitution constitute a grave evil in modern society'. Recognising the rapid growth of some economies in the post-war world, John XXIII in 1961 urged that class differences 'not be increased but lessened'. The Vatican Council in 1965 urged that 'the basic equality of all must receive increasingly greater recognition... For excessive economic and social differences between the members of the one human family... cause scandal, and militate against social justice, equity, the dignity of the human person, as well as social and international peace'. Criticisms of 'flagrant inequalities' have continued to be made since and there has been a growing appreciation of welfare state policies to ameliorate the worst inequalities.

Even when injustices have been acknowledged the response has tended to be the need for greater 'charity' and amelioration rather than prophetic challenge to break the chains which enslave so many people. On the whole there has been little serious social analysis of the structural causes of inequalities, except perhaps by liberation theologians, and relatively little in the way of concrete proposals to address the issue. What is needed is a serious scriptural and theological reflection on equality in the light of the scriptural account of the creation of all human beings in the 'image of God'. The scandal of social exclusion desperately needs a prophetic response from your generation. How will you respond?

5. Environmental Sustainability

As has happened several times during the writing of this book, some item of current news or an analysis of what is going wrong seems unusually relevant and indeed providential. Yesterday in the *Observer*, for example, there was an anguished appeal from a scientist for politicians, business people and indeed all of us as consumers, to wake up and for once take a longer term view of one of the major issues facing the whole world today. He started out by observing that it took 200,000 years for the global population to reach one billion but that at the current rate of growth the world's population is growing by one billion every decade and could well reach ten billion by the end of the century. But the article was not just about population numbers but about our consumption expectations, especially regarding water, food and energy. With increasing population more food will have to be produced. To feed ourselves over the next 40 years we will need to produce more food than we have in the past 10,000 years combined. 'Yet food productivity is set to decline... over the coming decades due to: climate change; soil degradation and desertification...; and water stress. By the end of this century, large parts of the planet will not have any usable water'. The consequence will be millions of 'climate migrants' with all the stress and antagonism that will cause. One estimate is that there will be 150 million 'environmental refugees' by 2050. Another strong possibility is a global pandemic.

The behavioural changes required of us in the west and north of the globe are so fundamental that no one is prepared to make them. We need to consume a lot less food, energy, and consumer goods generally. The science points to our being in 'an unprecedented emergency. We urgently need to do... something radical to avert a global catastrophe'. If you think the writer of the article is going 'over the top' look up on the internet the reports of the Intergovernmental Panel on Climate Change (IPCC) and the Stern Report in this country. If there is one thing which is apparent about our democratic political system it is that it is driven by short-term interests and concerns about the next election. It requires prophetic persistence and courageous commitment to take on these powers and interests in favour of long-term policies favouring the global common good, including future generations. That is a task which some of your generation will have to take on.

The seventh millennium development goal aimed to ensure environmental sustainability. There have been a number of high profile disasters in recent decades. Smoke emission from coal-fired power stations in Britain destroyed forests in Scandinavia. In 1986 the world's worst nuclear power accident at Chernobyl resulted in radioactive materials blowing north to Belarus which was declared an international ecological disaster zone. Cancer rates increased one hundred fold. Logging and deforestation in the Himalayas have resulted in flooding in Bangladesh. Disasters such as these have consequences which cross national borders and clearly point to the need for international regulation and response. There are huge inequalities in the consumption of non-replaceable resources. For example the US consumes around five times and the UK around two and a half times the world average use of commercial energy and electrical power consumption per capita. As a result of global warming sea levels are predicted to rise by up to a meter and several islands in the Indian and Pacific oceans will disappear. There will be 'more frequent and intense floods and droughts' and significant impacts on health.

An old interpretation of Genesis 1 was that human beings exercise 'domination' over the earth and that this legitimated the exploitation of the environment. The alternative view, which can be seen as a development of doctrine, favours an orientation of 'stewardship' of God's creation so that it is sustained and passed on to future generations in at least as healthy a state as it was received. Thus the bishops of England and Wales identified four main problems: damage to the earth's life-sustaining mechanisms, depletion of the world's natural resources, a harmful and unjust impact on the world's poor, and the loss of beauty and diversity. Seeking understanding of the 'signs of the times' they suggested that 'the environmental crisis has revealed the interdependence of all creation' and called for 'ecological conversion' because 'man is no longer the Creator's "steward" but an autonomous despot'.

They suggested that creation had value in itself and was 'good' and revealed God's generosity, majesty, and healing, nourishing and life-giving properties. Human beings were dependent but had the special gift and challenge of sharing responsibility in God's creative activity. But creation also revealed human sin which had distorted the human relationship with the natural world. Catholics were called to 'renew the face of the earth' until there was peace and harmony. In responding to the cry of creation they were called to take up personal responsibilities, educate towards ecological responsibility, experience conversion and choose not to consume what was not needed and what was likely to harm others, act in partnership and solidarity with others, aware that individual and collective greed were contrary to the order of creation.

The US bishops also called for 'an increased sense of stewardship'. They pleaded that 'the environmental crisis of our day constitutes an exceptional call to conversion' and reiterated that we are stewards of the earth 'charged with restoring the integrity of all creation'. They suggested that integral dimensions of ecological responsibility included a God-centred and sacramental view of the universe; a consistent respect for life; the affirmation of global interdependence and the common good; an ethic of solidarity; an understanding of the universal purpose of created things; an option for the poor; a conception of authentic development; and the restraint of the voracious consumerism of the developed world. This is quite a task for the follower of Jesus, of whom I hope you are one!

6. Authentic Development

A sixth area of concern is that of international distributive justice and what recent popes have called 'authentic development' in all its 'economic, social, cultural and spiritual aspects', that is more than just economic growth. A UN Human Development Report noted that 'the richest 5 percent of the world's people receive 114 times the income of the poorest 5 per cent. The richest 1 per cent receive as much as the poorest 57 percent'. And the evidence is that the gap has widened in recent years. Attention has moved from the amelioration of need to the search for understanding the root causes of persistent needs and injustices, now regarded as social and structural sins, and to social action such as political advocacy to change unjust structures.

As we noted in Letter 2 at a Millennium Summit in 2000 the UN committed themselves to seven Millennium Goals and various targets aimed to reduce global poverty by 2015. An eighth goal aimed to achieve these goals by means of a 'global partnership for development'. Trends over the past decade have not been very encouraging. Among the many concerns which illustrate the inequalities of power and vulnerability between nations are access to oil, food production and distribution, access to safe water supplies, access to cheap drugs and conflicts with powerful pharmaceutical corporations over 'intellectual property rights', and the management of debt. What seems apparent is that the less developed countries are excluded from full participation in the life of the global community in ways which are an offence to the values of human dignity, the common good and solidarity between nations.

Development is an extremely complex matter and there are opposing theories which attempt to explain inequalities of wealth, income and power between nations and why so many people in developing countries are so poor. The advocates of neo-liberal capitalism, which have included US dominated institutions such as the IMF, WB and WTO, have attributed global inequality and poverty to different levels of technological development and traditionalism in the prevailing cultures. These views glossed over power inequalities between nations, historical colonial linkages and dependencies, cultural ethnocentrism and a tendency to blame the victims. The alternative perspective attributed global inequality to the historical exploitation of poor countries by rich nations and new forms of economic neo-colonialism. On the other hand this tended to neglect factors internal to poor societies such as cultures resistant to change, gender inequality, political corruption and the reckless misuse of available resources.

The evidence does not support the unsubstantiated faith in 'trickle down' economics and many of the policies of the western dominated IMF and WB. A large number of developing nations, including Brazil, China, India and South Africa challenged western nations about the harmful impact to them of the $1 billion farm subsidies given each day by western countries to their farmers. Market fundamentalism has often been forced on poor nations while rich nations break rules with huge subsidies to cotton workers in the USA and sugar beet growers in the EU. These subsidies have devastating effects in developing nations, undercutting their crops and forcing them out of business. The granting by the WTO of 'intellectual property rights' to large corporations based in rich countries has been estimated to cost poor nations $40 billion a year.

Critical but pragmatic responses to present inequalities and injustices between rich and powerful nations, on the one hand, and poor and weak nations, on the other, are consistent with Christian approaches which acknowledge the sinfulness of humankind but also their striving towards that kingdom of justice and peace which will never be completely realised in this life but which Christians believe will be reached at the end of time.

Pope John XXIII in 1961 was the first pope to consider development issues seriously. He expressed concern at 'the relationship between economically advanced commonwealths and those that are in the process of development'. He was aware that aid by itself would not tackle the 'underlying causes of poverty and hunger' and advocated increasing international cooperation and a recognition of the growing interdependence of the peoples of the world. There has been a considerable development of teaching in the half century since then. The Second Vatican Council warned that economic development often 'serves only to intensify inequalities'. It recalled the saying of Gratian: 'Feed the man dying of hunger, because if you have not fed him you have killed him'.

Paul VI (1967) again pointed to 'the scandal of glaring inequalities' and introduced the Christian vision of 'authentic development' in all its 'economic, social, cultural and spiritual aspects'. He observed that we have inherited from the labours of past generations, benefited from our contemporaries and have obligations towards all, including future generations, in solidarity. Authentic development implied the transition from less human to more human conditions and was promoted by love, friendship, prayer and contemplation. Less human conditions arose where there was individual selfishness and 'oppressive social structures' and an absence of 'cooperation for the common good'. He condemned 'excessive inequalities of economic power' which resulted in increasing inequalities and appealed to all people of good will to live 'more fraternally' and work for development which was at the service of everyone for 'the new name for peace is development'.

Reviewing developments two decades later, John-Paul II (1987) noted the 'widening of the gap' between the developed North and developing South and suggested that both liberal capitalism and Marxist collectivism tended to be 'forms of neo-colonialism' fostering 'wars by proxy' which generated millions of refugees. Apart from poverty he also drew attention to the prevalence of unemployment and underemployment and the problem of international debt. A naive Enlightenment notion of 'progress' was unfounded and alongside the miseries of underdevelopment was to be found an 'inadmissible' form of 'super-development', consumerism, waste, and 'crass materialism'. Today's development began at the creation and was 'constantly endangered... by the temptation to idolatry'. The two typical structures of sin, 'the all-consuming desire for profit... (and) the thirst for power' were moral evils which needed to be confronted. He called for a spiritual conversion, a greater sense of moral responsibility and solidarity, the preferential option for the poor, and a recognition that 'the goods of this world are originally meant for all'. He called for reform of the international trade system, the world monetary and financial system and the question of technological exchanges.

In 2009 Benedict XVI returned to the theme of 'integral human development' and reflected at length on the themes of 'love' and 'gift' or the principle of gratuitousness which is an expression of fraternity. Reviewing developments in the four decades since Paul VI's encyclical he noted the growth of speculative financial dealing, large-scale migration, the unregulated exploitation of resources, the scandal of glaring inequalities, rigid intellectual property claims, the growing limitations to the economic sovereignty of states and the consequences of the deregulation of the labour market. There was a need to tackle short-termism and the structural causes of injustice and to 'cultivate a public conscience that considers food and access to water as universal rights of all... without discrimination'. The pope urged that 'a sustained commitment is needed... to promote a person-based and community-oriented cultural process of world-wide integration that is open to transcendence' steering 'the globalisation of humanity in relational terms of communion and the sharing of goods.' There needed to be a reconstruction of the international social order so that it at last conforms to the moral order.

I hope you find the developing teaching of these three popes inspiring and that you are challenged to make your own response to the glaring international inequalities and injustices.

7. *War and Peace*

Finally let us consider the frightening issues of war and peace. You may not have experienced the horrors of war in our own country during your lifetimes. But even so, we have experienced the serious terrorist bombings in London in 2005 and other terrorist incidents such as the recent killing of a soldier at Woolwich. And our armed forces have in recent years been involved in major wars in Iraq and Afghanistan. As I write this section there are reports of another drone attack in Pakistan which has killed many people. Within a year or so the issue of the updating of our Trident nuclear submarine system and the nuclear deterrence strategy will again be seriously considered.

The ending of the 'cold war' between the West and the Soviet Union has not meant the end of war. Extreme levels of inequality, communal injustices, or structural sins, inevitably generate grievances and conflicts which frequently lead to war. It is perhaps important to realise that recent terrorist atrocities, or 'asymmetric wars', appear to have been provoked by a sense of grievance against the power of the West and its arrogance and seeming indifference to the plight of billions of poor people in the developing world. Wars have been fought over access to vital raw materials such as oil and it seems a serious possibility that in the future there will be wars over access to clean water. So one important element in any Catholic position is the need to understand the causes of conflicts in structural injustices and sin.

Catholic social thought about war in a sinful world where conflict is endemic holds that war is not inevitable and that the violence of war is subject to moral restraint. There are roughly three Christian positions: conscientious pacifism, selective pacifism and the 'just war' tradition. Jesus stood in the Jewish prophetic tradition of non-violent resistance to injustice and this line appeared to have been followed by the early Church. But following the recognition of Christianity by Constantine, the institutional Church developed 'an application of the law of love that permitted legitimate defence of the innocent against unjust aggression'. Later this developed into the just war tradition.

The just war tradition dates from the early Church Fathers Ambrose and Augustine who began to formulate conditions when it was right to make war in a just cause (*ius belli*) and for its pursuit (*ius in bello*). Seven criteria have been suggested for determining when and why recourse to war might be permissible:

- When there is a just cause;
- In pursuit of the common good by a competent authority;
- With due concern for comparative justice between the parties to a conflict;
- With the right intention, i.e. pursuit of peace and reconciliation;
- Only as a last resort after exhausting all peaceful alternatives;
- There must be a probability of success; and
- There must be proportionality of damage inflicted.

Two principles for the *conduct* of war are particularly relevant today given the enormous destructive potential of modern weapons:

- Proportionality (avoiding escalation of the conflict); and
- Discrimination to ensure that the innocent (e.g. children) are not harmed, or in modern parlance 'collateral damage' is minimised.

It was for this reason that the Second Vatican Council totally rejected policies of 'total war'. The issue of discrimination has become increasingly relevant with the steady erosion of the distinction between combatants and non-combatants. Whereas only 5 per cent of those who died in the First World War were civilians, this increased to 66 per cent in the Second World War and is generally thought to be well over 90 per cent in recent wars such as Afghanistan.

With the coming of the industrial state, conscript armies, and especially weapons of mass destruction in the twentieth century, and more recently the use of pilotless drones to assassinate suspects, the Church has had to confront a totally new context. Though the traditional just war position has not been abandoned, the Second Vatican Council's unequivocal condemnation of modern 'total war', based on traditional just war principles, was perhaps a sign of the way Catholic social thought on war was going.

Recent Church thinking on the issues of war and peace in the era of nuclear weapons of mass destruction and chemical and biological weapons date from Pope John XXIII's encyclical *Pacem in Terris* (1963) and the Second Vatican Council's *Gaudium et Spes* (1965). Pope John stressed the need for nation states to regulate their relationships in accordance with 'the requirements of the universal common good'. He insisted that 'the same natural law, which governs relations between individual human beings, serves also to regulate the relations of nations with one another'. He pleaded for an end to the arms race and an effective programme of disarmament and 'a peaceful adjustment of relations between political communities on a world level... founded on mutual trust, on sincerity in negotiations, on faithful fulfilment of obligations assumed'. He suggested it was 'contrary to reason to hold that war is now a suitable way to restore rights which have been violated'. This required a public authority, such as the UNO, 'having worldwide power... set up by common accord and not imposed by force'.

Vatican II's *Gaudium et Spes* gave a flavour of the way the Church's teaching was developing. For the first time it recognised the right of conscientious objection and rejected 'blind obedience' to orders from superiors. It pointed out that 'peace is not merely the absence of war... (but) results from that harmony built into human society by its divine Founder, and actualised by men as they thirst after ever greater justice'. It warned that modern weapons 'can inflict massive and indiscriminate destruction far exceeding the bounds of legitimate defence'. Accordingly it declared explicitly against total war: 'Any act of war aimed indiscriminately at the destruction of entire cities or of extensive areas along with their population is a crime against God and man himself. It merits unequivocal and unhesitating condemnation'. It bemoaned the 'extravagant sums' spent on the arms race and looked forward to time when 'war can be completely outlawed by international consent'.

The Church continues to be ambivalent about the morality of nuclear deterrence but there is a growing sense that it can no longer be tolerated but must be rejected. This can be seen in the steady shift from John Paul II's acceptance of it as an interim measure 'towards a progressive disarmament' in 1982 to Cardinal Danneels emphatic statement in 1998 that 'nuclear weapons, whether used or threatened, are grossly evil and morally wrong. As an instrument of mass destruction, nuclear weapons slaughter the innocent and ravage the environment'. Steadily the Church seems to be moving towards a 'preferential option for non-violence'.

There is a multitude of issues which challenge the Christian conscience, including the often malicious effects of the arms trade, the morality of nuclear deterrence, intervention where there is genocide or civil war, the proper response to terrorist acts, and the morality of drones. All these issues will have to be addressed by you as a voting citizen in the years ahead. How are you going to work for a world where disputes can be resolved peacefully by international agreement?

8. Concluding Reflections

So, we must ask ourselves whether we are happy simply to be a 'poor, wee, cowering, timorous beastie', as Robert Burns put it, intimidated by the realities of social and economic power in our world? Or do we want to confront and challenge the sinful structures which are responsible for the grave injustices which exist both in our own society and also between nations in the wider world? In this letter I have outlined Catholic social teaching on a wide range of issues from human rights and family issues, through the range of economic issues such as social exclusion, environmental sustainability and authentic development, to those of war and peace. We have seen how the Church's teaching has developed from an awareness of God's purposes in creating us and the world we live in and in the light of twenty centuries of reflection on the teaching of Jesus and its application to the many issues which simply were not around in His world. Perhaps it all seems a bit 'heavy' for you at the moment but I am sure you will agree that there really are serious matters which your generation will have to address in the years ahead. As a responsible person you cannot simply look the other way. So how do you think you might contribute to the task facing the followers of Jesus?

Part IV

Social Action

Letter 8

Responding Individually

We now come to the final part of this book. So far we have looked in Part I at the social reality of the world you live in, both domestically in the UK and internationally in the globalised and increasingly interdependent world. We then suggested in Part II an interpretation of this world and noted the concentrations of social, economic, cultural and military power and the dominance of liberal capitalism and its various institutions. Thirdly, in Part III we brought to bear Christian perspectives and in particular the developing thinking of the Catholic Church on these issues, looking at seven areas in particular. Our task in this final Part IV of this book is to challenge you as to what responses you could make to the inequalities and injustices that exist both in our own country and in the globalised world in the light of the social and Christian analyses we have briefly outlined. In this letter I propose to consider what responses you might make as an individual and raise the issue of a challenging counter-culture and the role of prophecy. In Letter 9 I will focus on the possibilities of working in solidarity with others, for example in the wide range of campaigning groups.

1. Has Any One Wept?

Following the pattern I have used throughout the writing of this book, I would like to start this difficult task of inviting you to consider your response to the injustices and inequalities briefly outlined in this book by referring to the remarkable and challenging homily given by Pope Francis recently during the open-air Mass on the Italian island of Lampedusa. It is worth reading it in full and I suggest you might like to look it up on the internet.[7] The pope travelled to the small island around 75 miles from Tunisia where thousands of African migrants seeking a better life have landed. But the sea is treacherous and it is estimated that as many as 20,000 have lost their lives at sea in recent decades. Indeed, shortly before my revision of this letter there was another terrible loss of life off the island.

Pope Francis started by quoting the two questions asked by God early in Genesis: 'Adam, where are you?' after Adam's thinking he could be powerful and able to control everything and be God. And secondly, 'Cain, where is your brother?' after his murder of his brother, 'the other', someone who disturbed his life and comfort. The illusion of being powerful leads to a whole series of errors and a chain of death. The pope asked whether we, too, 'have lost our bearings; we are no longer attentive to the world in which we live; we don't care; we don't protect what God has created for everyone, and we end up unable even to care for one another! ...How often do such people (as the migrants) fail to find understanding, ...acceptance, ...solidarity?'

The pope challenged: 'Today no one in our world feels responsible; we have lost a sense of responsibility for our brothers and sisters.' Like the priest and levite in the parable of the Good Samaritan (Lk 10:29-37), we say 'It's not our responsibility.' There is a '*culture of comfort* which makes us

---

7 In www.Zenit.org for 8 July, 2013.

think only of ourselves, and makes us insensitive to the cries of other people.' He suggested that we live in 'bubbles which, however lovely, are insubstantial; they offer a fleeting and empty illusion which results in indifference to others; indeed it leads to the *globalisation of indifference.* In this globalised world we have fallen into globalised indifference. We have become used to the suffering of others; it doesn't affect me; it doesn't concern me; it is none of my business!' Pope Francis continued: 'We are a society which has forgotten how to weep, how to experience compassion, "suffering with others": the globalisation of indifference has taken from us the ability to weep! ...Let us ask the Lord for the grace to weep over our indifference, to weep over the cruelty of our world, of our hearts, and of all those who in anonymity make social and economic decisions which open the door to tragic situations' such as the deaths of would-be migrants.

What is your response to this challenging assessment of where we are? Do you care? Do you think the problems of this world are not your responsibility? Are you comfortable with the way things are? Are you indifferent to the world around you and the levels of inequality and injustices which exist? Do you think they are none of your business? Do you experience compassion for those who are suffering? What do you think you might do about it?

When I briefly described to some friends what I was trying to do in this book they challenged me: 'Have you bothered to ask your grandchildren what are the issues which bother them?' So at a family party the following weekend I asked my two oldest grandchildren, aged 20 and nearly 18, and they both looked blank and were not enthused by my suggestion that they might like to read and comment on the draft of my book. 'How many pages would it have?', they asked!

A survey of 14-18 year old young people, or Generation A, by Britain Thinks, was reported recently in the *Observer,* in the context of 'accelerating job insecurity, deep cuts to the public sector, flatlining salaries, rising housing costs and fierce competition, exacerbated by globalisation'. It was suggested that this generation might be one which 'for the first time will see some members slipping down the ladder of mobility and dying younger and possibly poorer than their parents'. Yet it was suggested that your generation was singularly well-equipped for the task and manifested resilience, pragmatism and humanity. Mm! I'm not so sure. The broad trends of declining social mobility and increasing inequality were confirmed by Alan Milburn's Commission report on Social Mobility and Child Poverty (October 2013). It all sounds rather worrying for you.

What strikes me every day as I read the evidence of increasing inequalities and injustices and the structural arrangements which seem to protect the rich and wealthy but damn the poor and weak, and the evidence of increasing control of our lives by a secretive and sometimes mendacious State, is what a sad state we are in. So what can we do about it? What do you think? Are you happy to let things work themselves out, hoping for the best, or do you think there is something rotten at the heart of our world which needs to be confronted and challenged? The choice is and will be yours.

2. Jesus' Call to Follow Him

At Mass on the morning I started writing this section, we heard the story of those towns, Chorazin, Bethsaida and Capernaum, which Jesus castigated because they had not responded positively to the evidence of His healing, miracles and preaching which they had seen and heard (Lk 10:13-15). Basically three types of response were identified: refusal to repent and accept Jesus' teaching, reluctance to do so because it would upset a cosy pattern of life, and indifference to its message. It was suggested that privileges, such as hearing God's word directly, gave responsibilities to respond; there were also the sins of indifference and of 'doing nothing'. How do you respond to Jesus' call to follow Him? What difference will it make to the way you get on with your life?

In spite of the immensity of the tasks to be addressed, there is the reassurance in the parable of the mustard seed (Lk 13:18-19) that even small contributions grow. Basically the spreading of God's kingdom on earth is God's gift which requires our cooperation and response. So how can we respond? Followers of Jesus are called to be 'mediators of God's saving activity' as servants for all people and with the aim of restoring relationships with God, humankind and creation. The realisation of the kingdom values of truth, life, justice, love, peace and joy would be truly world-transforming both in terms of personal relationships between people but also at the level of socio-economic structures. Scripture urges the restoration of Covenant relationships and the inclusion of the poor, weak and marginalised. The realisation of these kingdom values demands our conversion from self-interest and greed for wealth or power.

So where do you start? Nearly all those involved in the justice and peace movement are primarily concerned with a single issue of injustice. For example, many people are attracted to support campaigns for human rights promoted by Amnesty International. Others notice one of CAFOD's campaigns in their local parish and come to some awareness of development issues and injustices. Others in deprived inner-city areas strive to ensure that the voices of the poor are heard, the homeless cared for, or racism combated. Feminists seek to raise consciousness about the injustices experienced by women. Yet others are passionately concerned about peace issues and the arms trade. Every one of these issues is important as a matter of justice. As I have tried to indicate earlier in this book, they are all interlinked so that a greater awareness of the wider sinful structures which cause these injustices might be developed and lead to more insightful understanding and coordinated responses.

In the main, many injustices are the result of insufficiently regulated liberal capitalism so that the wealth and power of the rich and powerful individuals and commercial enterprises are reinforced and the gap between rich and poor people and nations is enhanced. Superimposed on this is the continuing legacy of former colonial exploitation. Globalising processes have failed to reduce economic inequalities and asymmetries of power which are essentially undemocratic and unjust. Present economic and political arrangements fail to express the values of equal human dignity and the common good. If we Christians are seriously seeking to advance the kingdom of God, here on earth as in heaven, then we must strive to reform the institutional arrangements in which so many of us have such a comfortable stake.

One example which comes to mind is that the older generations benefitted hugely from house price inflation in the 1990s and up to the credit crunch. This was partly due to a scandalous failure to build sufficient numbers of affordable homes. To these generations, anything which is likely to reduce house price inflation, such as more housing to reduce scarcity, is contested by the so-called 'nimbies' ('not in my backyard'). The result is that your generation is having great difficulty getting into the housing market.

The important thing is for you to select one issue which is meaningful to you and make a start, allowing an awareness of the wider issues to grow and develop and inspire from you an even greater response and commitment.

3. Challenging the Prevailing Culture: The Call to Prophecy

Over forty years ago Pope Paul VI in his 'call to action' acknowledged the variability of different social and cultural situations and the difficulty of putting forward solutions which have universal validity. Hence he urged local Christian communities to analyse the situation in their own country and, in dialogue with others of good will, to determine what responses were appropriate in order to bring about the social, political and economic changes necessary to produce greater social justice. So what needs to be done in our own society to change sinful social structures?

For the Christian the most important commandment is to love. True love brings conversion and an awareness of the need for that love to be realised effectively through structural changes, such as legislative regulation, which will almost certainly hurt some personal interests. Everyone has the ability to act; it is a matter of choice. To act is to demonstrate conversion. Coercive power is sustained by the belief that nothing can be done, that there is 'no alternative', or 'you can't buck the market'!

A recurrent theme in the Old Testament is the imperative to seek justice, 'to do what is right' (Micah 6:8), 'to open the eyes of the blind, to free captives from prison, and those who live in darkness from the dungeon' (Isaiah 42:7), 'to sooth the broken-hearted, to proclaim liberty to captives, release those in prison, to proclaim a year of favour from Yahweh' (Isaiah 61:2). The Israelites were instructed not to 'cheat the poor... of their rights', 'oppress the alien' (Exodus 23: 6, 9) or exploit the weak or ill-treat the poor (Amos 4: 1). Justice was to be administered impartially (Leviticus 19: 15). Proper care had to be taken of 'the foreigner, the orphan and the widow' (Deuteronomy 14: 29), the weak and vulnerable.

This theme of justice-seeking, so easily overlooked in over-sentimental forms of spirituality ('Gentle Jesus meek and mild'), continues at the core of the teaching of Jesus. At the very beginning of his mission he announced that God had anointed him 'to bring the good news to the afflicted... to proclaim liberty to captives, sight to the blind, to let the oppressed go free, to proclaim a year of favour from the Lord' (Lk 4: 18), that is release from debt. When talking about true discipleship Jesus taught bluntly that 'it is not anyone who says to me "Lord, Lord", who will enter the kingdom of heaven, but the person who does the will of my Father in heaven' (Mt 7: 21). In his parable of the last judgement he taught that those called to the Kingdom would be those who had fed the hungry, given drink to the thirsty, welcomed the stranger, given clothes to those without, and to those who visited the sick and imprisoned (Mt 25: 31-46). St. James insisted that it was through deeds that faith was demonstrated and that 'it is by deeds, and not only by believing, that someone is justified' (Jas 2:14-26). St. Paul reminded that good works reflected the faith that had been given as a free gift (Eph 2: 7-10).

Pope Paul, drawing on the teaching of Vatican II, recalled that the laity 'should take up as their own proper task the renewal of the temporal order.' He continued: 'It is not enough to recall principles, state intentions, point to crying injustices, and utter prophetic denunciations; these words will lack real weight unless they are accompanied for each individual by a livelier awareness of personal responsibility and by effective action. It is too easy to throw back on others responsibility for injustices, if at the same time one does not realise how each one shares in it personally, and how personal conversion is needed first'.

The US bishops in 1986 admitted that 'the Gospel is demanding' and that 'conversion is a lifelong process'. They asked lay people 'to become more informed and active citizens, using your voices and votes to speak for the voiceless, to defend the poor and vulnerable and to advance the common good. We are called to shape a constituency of conscience, measuring every policy by how it touches the least, the lost, and the left-out among us... (They called) us to conversion and common action, to new forms of stewardship, service and citizenship'. This spelt out what was required not only from citizens of the nation state but also of the world. Christians were called to take the Good News to the poor, not only in their own country, but to all people on earth. Given the obscene inequalities of wealth in the world, it seemed appropriate to cultivate a more modest and egalitarian lifestyle.

What would that mean for you? Not having too much to drink on Saturday nights out? Not following temporary fashions of celebrities or buying the latest 'gadget'? Give it some serious thought.

At the same time it is necessary to be realistic. The kingdom of God, while here among those striving to do God's will, will only be fully realised at the end of time. That is God's work. The Christian is called to assist and not frustrate its achievement. What is condemned is apathy, indifference and self-satisfaction. The message to the Church in Laodicea is apposite: 'since you are neither hot nor cold, but only lukewarm, I will spit you out... so repent in real earnest' (Rev 3: 14-22). Christians must start where they are. The important thing is that everyone, including you, does something, marvelling, as St. Thérèse of Lisieux pointed out, at the contribution of 'little flowers' to the beauty of nature and the wider picture. As previously mentioned, the parable of the mustard seed (Lk 13:18-19) is relevant and encouraging. Contemporary examples of the success of small beginnings over time include the environmental movement and the campaign to cancel the debt of highly indebted poor countries.

To sum up this section, followers of Jesus are called to challenge the culture of complacency which accepts things as they are, as inevitable and natural. You are called, rather, to advocate an alternative, counter-culture which gives priority to the needs of the poorest and weakest and persistently advocates behaviour and social policies which support and encourage them. In other words, you are called to be prophets of a better way of life and human behaviour in a world which is largely run in the interests of the rich and powerful individuals and corporations and where the majority of people is largely indifferent.

4. Making a Start

So how do you do this and make a start? Among the tactics typically used by activists are marches and demonstrations, non-violent direct action, letter-writing, signing petitions, and political lobbying. There is something exciting and reassuring about going on a large demonstration, appreciating the support and solidarity of so many other people and making friendships which can sometimes last a life-time. I remember going to Greenham Common on a Good Friday morning in support of the women activists protesting against nuclear weapons. I was also on the huge anti-Iraq war march in 2003. I flew to and from Gatwick to take part in the great 'Make Poverty History' demonstration in Edinburgh in 2005 and I joined the large demonstration of environmental concern before the Copenhagen meeting in 2009. I can strongly recommend you keep your eyes open for such important demonstrations of concern with existing social policies. You will find them instructive, reassuring to become aware that so many others share your concerns, and invigorating and challenging to maintain your protests and campaigning. I never felt called to participate in the regular acts of non-violent direct action such as writing critical comments about Trident on the walls of the Ministry of Defence but I do admire those who keep raising such matters to the attention of a sleepy, indifferent and complacent general public.

These days there are numerous issues for which a multitude of campaigning groups attempt to challenge existing or proposed policies. Many campaigning groups, including well-known internet groups such as Avaaz, invite supporters to sign internet petitions or brief cards addressed to the prime minister, a government minister or the local M.P. Insiders testify that the weight or number of these cards or emails is taken seriously. MPs have said that they take particular notice when more than about twenty constituents express concern about a particular issue. It is certainly a relatively painless way of making a start. But again, it seems undoubtedly to be the case that a personal letter or email is taken much more note of than one of thousands of signed but similar reproduced cards. What is important is to begin with an issue which particularly grabs you, follow it up and try to inform yourself more thoroughly about the issue by joining a relevant campaigning group or looking up further information about the issue on the internet. It may even be worth exploring interest on the issue through social networking media.

It may be that there is a particularly significant local issue which is arousing much attention. Increasing numbers of homeless on the streets or people relying on food banks, or large numbers of migrant workers subject to violence or intimidation would be obvious examples. Remember, though, the pointed observation of the charismatic Brazilian bishop, Helder Camara, that 'when I feed the hungry they call me a saint, but when I ask why they are hungry, they call me a communist'. In other words the amelioration of obvious needs, such as feeding those in areas of famine, are socially approved of and relatively unproblematic. But it is when you ask what are the structural causes of persistent famine which might have something to do with climate changes or failure to allow access to water, or to the replacement of traditional farming methods by industrialised agriculture, or whatever, that then the likelihood is that you will be challenging powerful vested interests and generating hostility and public condemnation. You might also be fortunate enough to find an active local Amnesty International group or some keen environmentalists and conservationists. They all help you to make a start.

You might also be fortunate enough to live in a parish where there is a justice and peace group. There you will have the support of like-minded parishioners and friends. Groups typically meet monthly and arrange a cycle of events throughout the year to help raise awareness of the wide range of issues calling for some sort of Christian response. It would be useful, too, to develop a good relationship with those planning the weekly liturgies so that justice issues become totally integrated with the worship of the local parish community. Try to ensure that there is at least one bidding prayer each week which prays for a weak or oppressed group or a situation of injustice or current concern. If there isn't a parish J&P group you could always start one by personal invitation to those likely to be interested, or by putting a notice in the parish newsletter. Better still, you could ask the parish priest to invite parishioners to join a J&P group in a spoken appeal at the end of Mass, or even better, allow you to speak briefly yourself. The aim is to raise awareness that justice is 'no optional extra' but an integral part of our lives as followers of Jesus.

The range of concerns is so wide that no individual or small group can hope to address them all. Members of a parish J&P group will bring their own pet concerns. But one possible framework broadly speaking starts after the summer holidays and commences in September with Racial Justice Sunday. A simple but very effective arrangement is to invite around eight to ten individuals with different first languages to give a one or two-sentence welcome in their language of origin along the lines: 'You are all welcome here on Racial Justice Sunday and we invite you to share in and celebrate the marvellous diversity in our parish community.' If you have a lively Children's Liturgy Group they could be involved, for example by getting the children to bring up with the offertory gifts, the flags of their countries of origin. In previous weeks parishioners could be invited to stick pins on a map of the world, or Europe, indicating their place of birth. These are all marvellous demonstrations of the cultural diversity and the universality of the Church and an invitation to work together in harmony.

As Christmas approaches you might consider inviting parishioners to recommend a charity for special consideration. In our parish we call this the '10% collection' because we invite parishioners to contribute 10% of their total Christmas spending towards the charities voted for by the parishioners. We have sometimes selected one local, one national and one international charity. Preparation for this must begin around late September or early October by inviting parishioners to propose a worthy charity of their choice. The J&P group should prepare guidelines as to what information is necessary about the recommended charity. This needs to be repeated over several weeks until parishioners are invited to vote on their preferred choices no later than mid-November. Early in December abbreviated information about the chosen charities should be made available to parishioners along with gift-aided envelopes. Again reminders should be made over several weeks until early January and the allocated proceeds forwarded to the chosen charities as soon as possible.

Another pre-Christmas activity is the sending of greetings cards to international prisoners of conscience. Amnesty International around early December provides details of a score or so of selected prisoners with details of to whom the greeting might be sent and what wording might be appropriate and not offensive to local sensitivities. For example, the prisoners may not be Christian or they may be incarcerated in a Moslem country. Amnesty advises on such sensitivities. The J&P group could typically make available information sheets for about half a dozen selected prisoners and make available appropriate cards (such as accumulated unused charity cards and envelopes) and appropriate overseas stamps. Parishioners could be invited to complete the cards after Mass but they may prefer to do so later. Contributions to cover the cost of stamps could be suggested. If there are objections to using Amnesty International's name because of its recent policy on abortion, the J&P group could simply adapt the AI material. The important point is to show solidarity to the prisoners of conscience.

As soon as Christmas is over there is a particularly busy season. First of all Peace Sunday occurs in mid-January and the J&P group could invite some sort of reflection on the issues of war and peace in the modern era and also the issues raised by the global arms trade and the UK's particularly significant involvement in it. It is also a good opportunity to invite donations after Mass for Pax Christi which is not a charity and which relies heavily on parish contributions. No sooner is Peace Sunday over than we have the two Sundays at either end of Poverty and Homelessness Week when gift-aided collections for Church Action on Poverty and Housing Justice are particularly relevant. As I write this in the middle of a great recession there are serious warnings about the numbers of homeless and the squeezing of poor people's standard of living. For those in many inner-city areas this is an everyday experience but even in the comfy suburbs there is a need to raise awareness of the plight of those less fortunate than ourselves. Support might be given to local food banks or credit unions but it is particularly important to ask the justice question: why are things like this?

There are always other issues such as 'authentic development', climate change and environmental issues generally, the plight of migrant workers or the evils of child trafficking which could be the focus of attention raising during Lent or the Easter period depending on the particular interests of the J&P group's members. Key sources of information such as CAFOD or Progressio or Christian Ecology Link are well worth following up. Other key issues tend to fall during the summer holiday season and get ignored but the J&P group could make some arrangements to remember the anniversaries of the nuclear bombing of Hiroshima and Nagasaki early in August, for example. Finally, there are the periodic meetings of the G20 nations or key UN events which often give rise to international campaigning. So keep your eyes open for these.

Depending on your personal circumstances, the following ways are worth pursuing:

- Cultivate a spirituality of justice-seeking with regular reading of the scriptures. Become familiar with Catholic social thought.
- Join or start a parish justice and peace group. Ask your parish to sponsor your attendance at the annual National Justice and Peace Network (NJPN) conference.
- Start in a small way doing something such as letter-writing to your M.P. and participating in email campaigns.
- Join a group or campaigning organisation and gain encouragement, support and knowledge from others with similar concerns.
- Become an ethically conscious consumer aware of your lifestyle and consumer choices and support Traidcraft. Become an ethical investor and learn to monitor the claims of corporate social responsibility.
- Develop a concern for the environment by taking recycling and composting seriously and reducing energy and water consumption. Keep an eye open for campaigns about climate change.
- Seek relationships with marginalised and excluded people and consider volunteering for the local homeless refuge and supporting a local food bank or Credit Union.
- Participate in major demonstrations such as the recent IF campaign – if the world produces enough food for everyone, why are so many children still dying of hunger?
- Share gifts with those less fortunate such as CAFOD's and other charities' Christmas gifts of latrines, goats and water wells to change the lives of those living in poverty.

All of these actions contribute to the construction of a 'culture of life' and a strong 'civil society' imbued with a distinctive Christian morality and values, capable of challenging existing structures of power, seeking ways to alleviate suffering and need, constructing social policies which promote the dignity of each individual human person, and seeking the common good in solidarity with others. As Deuteronomy puts it: '...I have set before thee life and death, the blessing and the curse; therefore choose life'. So, 'choose life', start from where you are and do not be afraid of small beginnings.

5. Pick up Your Cross: It Will Not be Easy or Painless

As I suggested above, we are trying to create a challenging and prophetic counter-culture fundamentally at odds with a general assumption that the world is as good as it can be. We may be relatively comfortable and even well-off. But if we only open our eyes we can see that all is not well, either domestically or internationally in a globalised world. There are still millions of people who are starving while we are overeating. There are millions of refugees in a pitiful state in the world and most states, including our own, are hostile to them and to asylum seekers. Contrasts between the relative comfort of the developed nations and the rural poverty of millions in the developing nations are huge and it is no wonder that millions attempt to migrate in the hope of obtaining work and in order to support their families by working in relatively rich societies like ours. But such migrant workers are frequently discriminated against and often experience extreme levels of hostility. Money spent on the arms trade would be sufficient to end poverty in the developing world. And so on. The task of followers of Jesus is to challenge the culture of complacency and indifference and insist that a better way is possible and that we must offer a challenging counter-culture which respects the rights of every human individual and promotes the common good of all people in solidarity with all, especially the poor, weak and oppressed. So let us build a 'culture of life', as Pope John Paul II put it.

While it is true that every little 'mustard seed' can grow and that every contribution to seeking the justice of the kingdom of God is valuable, it is not the case that such work is without cost. The cross is at the heart of the Christian call to discipleship. Campaigning about justice and peace issues will not be easy and you will almost certainly face ridicule and, in some cases, discrimination and aggressive antagonism. It could be painful. After all, you will be challenging the wealthiest and most powerful interests not only in the land, but also, in the case of large multinational corporations, in the world. It wouldn't be easy, for example, to advocate a reduction of the arms trade in an area where a large proportion of the local workforce is employed on defence contracts! Or campaigning on behalf of illegal immigrants in some inner-city areas. Or urging reform of the EU Common Agricultural Policy in rural areas where large subsidies are being paid to local farmers. There are plenty of examples. Jesus did warn his followers that they would need to pick up their crosses and follow a sometimes difficult and thankless path. But he also reassured them that he would be with them on their journey in pursuit of the kingdom of God on earth as in heaven. We must be confident and reassured by Jesus' promise: 'Do not let your hearts be troubled... I am the Way; I am the Truth and life' (Jn 14: 1,6).

So, what are you waiting for? Now is the time to start. But you needn't be alone. Apart from your local parish justice and peace group there is a multiplicity of campaigning organisations which have expertise in specific areas and are experienced also in the various techniques of campaigning and lobbying decision makers. An outline of some of the major organisations and NGOs will be given in the following letter.

Letter 9

Responding In Solidarity

This book has followed a four-stage 'pastoral cycle' which suggests one way in which the follower of Jesus can attempt to respond to the inequalities and injustices which are apparent in the world in which we live. Firstly, we considered this social reality of our world both domestically and internationally. Secondly we attempted by means of social analysis to answer the questions 'why do these injustices occur? What are the main causes and who are the key powerful decision-makers?'. Thirdly, we sought to bring a Christian perspective to bear in particular looking at what scripture might tell us or what developments in Catholic social thought might suggest to us. The fourth stage of our 'pastoral cycle' challenges us to respond with some sort of ***social action***. In Letter 8 I focused in particular on the response of the individual follower of Jesus on his/her journey through life. S/he was called to challenge prophetically the prevailing culture. In this final letter I will focus primarily on what they can do in collaboration and solidarity with other activists and oppressed people in a wide range of campaigning organisations.

As I proceed with this final letter after our return from holiday, I will follow the general style I have adopted of a friendly letter from me to one of my grandchildren, making reference to something relevant in the contemporary news. Well, it so happens that the Gospel readings this week have been from Matthew Chs. 19 and 20. Yesterday we heard about the rich young man who confessed he had not broken any of the commandments but to justify himself asked Jesus what else he needed to do to merit eternal life. Jesus told him bluntly to sell all his goods and come and follow Him. I think all of us would have had difficulty responding to that challenge. Then today Jesus tells us how difficult it will be for the rich to enter the gates of the kingdom of heaven but while it might be impossible for man to enter through the 'eye of a needle', for God all things are possible. 'The first (the rich and powerful?) will be last and the last (the poor and oppressed?), first'. Then tomorrow, in the parable of the labourers in the vineyard, all get promised wages according to need rather than hours worked, something which offends our sense of fairness. In other words, God's ways are not our ways. There is much here to ponder as we try to sort out our own response to Jesus' call to follow Him.

In the previous letter I made some suggestions as to how each of us as individuals might make a start in taking 'the Good News to the poor'. In general terms, though, Christians are also called to work in collaboration with all people of good will, through the institutions of civil society - non-governmental organisations (NGOs), campaigning groups, voluntary organisations, and the like – to promote human flourishing, enhance human dignity, the common good and solidarity between all God's people and the integrity of the whole of God's creation. Followers of Jesus, pilgrims, servants and prophets, are called to work together and in solidarity with other activists and, perhaps most challenging, with the oppressed such as the poor and homeless, or with village farmers in developing societies. First we will consider working with other people of faith and in particular in a reformed servant Church as we experience this at the local parish level. Secondly, we will consider the vocation of Christians working in the public sector and especially politicians. Thirdly, we will review the wide range of campaigning groups covering the range of domestic and international concerns. Finally we will offer some final reflections on the daunting task of addressing the multitude of inequalities and injustices in our contemporary world and invite you to respond as the Lord would have you respond.

1. A Challenging and Prophetic Church

But first we might consider how the Church of Christ might best contribute towards this venture. Many of us in the older generations grew up in a clericalised Church which was hierarchical and somewhat authoritarian. Catholic action had to be under the control of the hierarchy. Things did begin to change with Pope John XXIII's 'breath of fresh air' and the Second Vatican Council in the 1960s. But many Catholic activists would judge that the process has since stalled somewhat and that the Catholic Church itself needs reforming in order to become more of a servant and less of a master. Pope Francis seems to favour a servant model of the Church. After all, Jesus did teach that the greatest among you must be your servant' (Mt 23:11) and Mark tells us that He told the twelve apostles: 'If anyone wants to be first, he must make himself last of all and servant of all' (Mk 9:35). At the Last Supper after the degrading experience of washing His disciples' feet He told them: 'If I, then, the Lord and Master, have washed your feet, you must wash each other's feet' (Jn 13:14). The signals coming from Pope Francis as I write are very encouraging.

The idea of the Church as servant was one of the five models which Avery Dulles examined a decade after Vatican II. With this model the Church would give 'hope in the ultimate coming of God's kingdom, and commitment to the values of peace, justice, and human brotherhood, all of which are dominant biblical themes'. He suggested that: 'A servant Church can effectively herald the gospel as a triumphal Church could not. Only in becoming a faithful servant of the Servant Lord can the Church effectively proclaim the good news of the Christian revelation'. These reflections challenge us to ask to what extent the Church is indeed a servant on the side of the poor, deprived and oppressed. A promising example was given recently by the Archbishop of Canterbury who spoke out strongly against the shameful and usurious interest rates charged by Wonga for unsecured short-term loans. This also led to a renewed interest in Credit Unions at the local level.

In many ways we are fortunate to have a recently elected Pope Francis who is offering signs of hope that the Church under his leadership might well be moving in this direction. In the previous letter I quoted his challenging homily at Lampedusa about the plight of would-be migrants from Africa. It remains to be seen to what extent the promising rhetoric is translated into action. The Roman Catholic Church is a powerful player on the international scene. To what extent does it forego cosy relationships with powerful secular elites in order to seek justice for the poor or oppressed? Do we yet have a challenging and prophetic Church?

At the diocesan level how much support is given to the Justice and Peace movement? Sadly, several dioceses in England and Wales have recently felt it necessary to make their J&P workers redundant in their attempts to achieve financial stability. When will there be a determined effort to give the pursuit of justice and peace a higher priority and provide it with appropriate resources? At the parish level, too, where is the evidence that the servant model of the Church is being promoted? A number of relevant suggestions were made in the previous letter. These include the setting up and encouragement of a parish Justice and Peace Group. Much can be achieved within the parish by way of raising awareness of current needs in weekly contributions to the bidding prayers. Close and friendly relations with the Liturgy Committee, or those responsible for the choice of hymns and so on, would be very helpful. Encouragement for the parish clergy to raise relevant concerns and preach about them in their scripture reflections and homilies would be useful ways of mobilising ordinary parishioners to the calls of the Lord.

The Second Vatican Council referred to the Church as 'the people of God'. All its members have their own talents and gifts which they are invited to contribute to the collaborative task of taking 'the good news to the poor'. The parish and its J&P group is one place where the individual can find support and solidarity with others in the pursuit of campaigns which can sometimes be unpopular. It is also the place where one can become most aware that Jesus who is 'the way, the truth and the life' (Jn 14: 6) promised to be with us 'always; yes to the end of time' (Mt 28: 20).

2. Christians in the Public Arena: Politics as a Vocation

Politicians have recently had a pretty bad press with concerns about the misuse of expenses and so on. Membership of the main political parties has plummeted in recent years as has the proportion of electors who bother to vote. There is a common view that 'they are only in this for their own purposes' and that it won't make any difference how you vote; in the end the same groups benefit and the rest of us pick up the pieces. There is a general cynicism about politics and politicians.

Interestingly, there have been a number of comments recently that have suggested a much more serious problem with contemporary politics. One obvious aspect is short-termism, the tendency to think only within the time-span to the next election, only a few years ahead. The danger with this is that the most serious and long-term issues are side-tracked and not seriously analysed, debated and acted upon. There are numerous examples of this. The issue of nuclear deterrence in a world where terrorism rather than inter-state conflicts are more likely is one. The issues of airport expansion and high-speed rail links would be others. Fundamental shifts in and the updating of the welfare state would be others. Coming to terms with the incredible increase in the average life expectancy and its implications for the long-term care of the elderly is an issue which is not easily addressed by short-term politics and decision-making. It also requires the mobilisation of opinion across party lines, a challenging task.

Internationally, there is a need to recognise the changing nature of the contemporary world decades after the post-World War II settlement and setting up of the UN Security Council. The USA, Britain and Russia may have been key players in the 1950s but the emergence of China, India, Brazil and other countries needs to be reflected in major changes in the United Nations Organisation and the composition of such major international institutions as the Security Council, the International Monetary Fund and the World Bank. In the case of the UK there is a need to acknowledge the importance of close relations with our nearest neighbours in Europe. All of these sorts of issue, domestic and international, tend to be ignored by the corrosive influence of short-termism in politics, the general cynicism about politics which is so prevalent today, and the failure to acknowledge the way the world, and our role in it, have changed over the past six decades.

Perceptive commentators have recently suggested more subtle changes taking place in contemporary politics. For example, there has been a decline in the class-based nature of politics, possibly reflecting massive changes in the nature of employment such as the decline in the proportion in manual work, the emergence of a property-owning democracy and the consequences of social mobility as a result of access to higher education. The slogans that 'we are all in this together' and 'we're all middle-class now' may be myths but they are very powerful myths. They do help explain the decline of class-based identifications and the stress towards maximising support from 'middle England'. It has resulted in a politics driven by the need to maximise support rather than pursue identifiably distinct agendas. The perception that political parties 'are all the same' has contributed to a general disillusionment with politics.

Against all these rather pessimistic views I would like to suggest we need a more positive approach to politics and to the vocation of the politician. The role of the politician is essential in a democratic society. Not only do politicians mediate between the electors and the Government decision-makers, but they also both articulate current concerns and propose various solutions to contemporary problems. This is an essential and sometimes thankless vocation. We should pray for our politicians that they will be guided to make judgements favouring the common good and always have a 'preferential option for the poor.'

So one of the first things I would suggest you consider seriously is whether to join a political party and participate actively in its various activities including the raising of awareness of major issues but also assisting in the formulation of policies in pursuit of the goals you feel are just and worthwhile. In this way you would be actively involved in seeking the 'kingdom of God on earth as in heaven'. The main problem will be to discern which political party is most likely to share your concerns for human dignity, the common good, subsidiarity, solidarity, the preferential option for the poor, and a preferential option for non-violence.

3. Campaigning Groups

This book has been drafted in the United Kingdom so that most of the suggestions made will relate to UK campaigning groups. But where possible and given the possibility that this book might have a wider readership, I would like to draw attention to similar organisations elsewhere and in particular Australia and the United States. In the United States, the Center of Concern in Washington DC has a very broad reach across all the areas of injustice mentioned in this book. Note also in the cyber age the power of such campaigning groups as Avaaz and SomeOfUs which are international in their reach.

The following suggestions represent a fraction of those organisations and campaigning groups working in the seven broad areas of justice outlined in this book. Unless stated otherwise, these organisations all operate in the UK. The outlines I have given below have for the most part been taken from their websites or Wikipedia. Up to date information on all of them can be found in these sources. Those listed are, for the most part, campaigning groups which publish appropriate research or informational materials rather than charities mainly concerned with the amelioration of need.

(a) Human Rights Concerns

Amnesty International:

This is a worldwide movement whose members campaign for internationally recognized human rights to be respected and protected. It works to protect individuals wherever justice, fairness, freedom and truth are denied. It campaigns for the abolition of the death penalty, for a fair and effective asylum system, and against forced eviction. It also works on a wide range of issues such as bringing the arms trade, which fuels conflict, poverty and human rights abuses worldwide, under control. Members exert influence on governments, political bodies, companies and intergovernmental groups, not only through various communications and media channels but also by mobilizing public pressure through mass demonstrations, vigils and direct lobbying.

Freedom from Torture (formerly Medical Foundation for the Care of Victims of Torture)

This organisation solely treats victims of torture. Since it was established in 1985 over 50,000 people have been referred to the organisation for help. It provides medical and psychological documentation of torture, a range of therapies including individual and family counselling and group work as well as practical advice and support. It trains health professionals throughout the UK to work with torture survivors. A key area of work is educating the public and decision-makers about torture and its consequences, and advocacy on behalf of torture survivors with the aim of keeping the issue on the national agenda.

Jesuit Refugee Service

The JRS is an international Catholic organisation with a mission to accompany, serve and advocate on behalf of refugees and other forcibly displaced persons. Founded in 1980 it has programmes in 50 countries. It provides assistance to refugees in camps and cities, individuals displaced within their own countries, asylum seekers in cities, and those held in detention centres. The main areas of work are in the field of education, emergency assistance, healthcare, livelihood activities and social services. It is also concerned with advocacy and human rights work to ensure refugees are afforded their full rights while in exile and during repatriation. It lobbies for and promotes international human rights legislation.

Liberty (formerly the National Council for Civil Liberties)

Founded in 1934 it is a cross-party and non-party membership movement for fundamental rights and freedoms. It promotes the values of human dignity, equal treatment and fairness as the foundation of a democratic society. It campaigns to protect basic rights and freedom through the courts, in Parliament and in the wider community. It does this through a combination of public campaigning, test case litigation, parliamentary lobbying, public analysis and the provision of free advice and information.

Migration Policy Group (Brussels)
Located in Brussels, the MPG is an independent think tank established in 1995 which is committed to achieving lasting progress towards a more open and inclusive European society in which all members, with or without an immigrant background, have equal rights, responsibilities and opportunities and a commitment to contribute to the economic, social, cultural and civic life of our diverse societies. It pursues this through quality independent research, expert policy analysis, network building, advocacy, benchmarking and training.

Prison Reform Trust
Established in 1981 by a small group of prison reformers, it aims to create a just, humane and effective penal system. It aims to improve prison regimes and conditions, defend and promote prisoners' human rights, address the needs of prisoners' families, and promote alternatives to custody. It carries out research on all aspects of prison and its activities include advice and information, education and parliamentary lobbying.

Refugee Council
This organisation has been working with refugees and people seeking asylum for over 60 years. It offers practical support and advice throughout their journey in the UK and has a thorough understanding of the difficulties facing people arriving in the UK, with unimaginable stories to tell, having fled war, rape, and torture. Many refugees have lost everything and their lives will never return to normal. The Refugee Council offers a helping hand to support and empower them to rebuild their lives.

(b) The Family And Bioethical Issues

The Anscombe Bioethics Centre (formerly the Linacre Centre for Healthcare Ethics)
This charity, founded in 1977, is a Roman Catholic academic institute that engages with the moral questions arising in

clinical practice and biomedical research. It brings to bear on those questions the principles of natural law, virtue ethics, and the teaching of the Catholic Church, and seeks to develop the implications of that teaching for emerging fields of practice. The Centre engages in scholarly dialogue with academics and practitioners of other traditions. It contributes to public policy debates as well as debates and consultations within the Church. It runs educational programmes for, and gives advice to, Catholics and other interested healthcare professionals and biomedical scientists.

Life

Through its network of Care Centres, its National Helpline or its Text or Talk service, LIFE Care provides non-directive counselling and support for anyone facing an unplanned pregnancy, suffering the loss of a baby or coping after abortion. Life is a pro-life charity that supports anyone facing such a crisis situation and strives to engage, inspire and inform the next generation and prevent teenage pregnancies. It also houses women and children fleeing domestic violence.

Society for the Protection of the Unborn Child (SPUC)

SPUC is a pro-life organisation which opposes abortion, assisted suicide, some forms of birth control and same sex marriage. It affirms, defends and promotes the existence and value of human life from the moment of conception and aims to defend and protect human life generally. It reasserts the principle laid down in the UN Declaration of the Rights of the Child that the child 'needs special safeguards and care, including appropriate legal protection, before as well as after birth.' It aims to defend, assist and promote the life and welfare of mothers during pregnancy and of their children from the time of conception up to, during and after birth. It examines and campaigns about existing or proposed laws, legislation or regulations relating to abortion.

(c) Economic Life

Ecumenical Council for Corporate Responsibility (ECCR)

ECCR is a church-based investor coalition, registered charity and membership organisation which leads and collaborates with others in advocacy and awareness raising on issues of business, human rights and environmental stewardship. It has filed shareholder resolutions, raised concerns with and engaged in dialogue with companies and leading fund managers and institutional investors, on a range of issues. It has made submissions to the UK Government, European Parliament and International Labour Organisation. Its British, Irish and international members include representatives of many Christian denominations, faith-based investors, religious communities and orders, non-governmental organisations, ethical investment managers and committed individuals.

Ethical Investment Research Service (EIRIS)

EIRIS is an independent, not-for-profit organisation which helps clients develop the market in ways that benefit investors, asset managers and the wider world. Its mission is to empower responsible investors with independent assessments of companies' environmental, social governance (ESG) performance and advice on integrating them with investment decisions. It provides responsible investment services to asset owners and managers, banks, stock brokers and governments around the world, as well as major index providers. It has 30 years experience of promoting responsible investment and helping global investors, consumers, charities and financial advisors to invest responsibly. A recent addition to its global research is Conflict Risk Network.

International Christian Union of Business Executives (UNIAPAC)

UNIAPAC originated in 1931 as a federation of associations of Christian business leaders in Western Europe. In 1962 it became an ecumenical association and currently has members in 33 countries and four continents. It welcomes membership associations, individual members and companies worldwide. Its aims include the study, maintenance and propagation of the principles and applications of Christian social thought.

New Economics Foundation (NEF)
The NEF is a British think-tank founded in 1986 with the motto 'economics as if people and the planet mattered'. It worked for a new model of wealth creation based on equality, diversity and economic stability. Its programmes include work on well-being, new kinds of measurement and evaluation, sustainable local regeneration, new forms of finance and new business models, sustainable public services, and the economics of climate change.

World Movement of Christian Workers (WMCW)
The WMCW was set up in 1966. Today it brings together more than 70 affiliated organisations from four continents. Its member organisations promote the interests of all those who rely on their work for their income. It is a movement of formation through action. The member movements are committed to raising awareness through permanent education. Their objective is to create solidarity and encourage their members to take an active part in the commitment to social change using the 'see-judge-act' or 'review of life' method. The ultimate goal of this collective action of continuing education is to improve the living conditions of all workers and their families. It calls upon its members to give a political dimension to their commitment. Its inspiration is the Gospel which invites us to make a preferential option for the poor, the vulnerable and the excluded.

(d) Social Exclusion

ATD Fourth World
This international movement was founded in Paris in 1957 and today operates in eight European countries, Northern and

Central America, and several countries in Africa and Asia. It has three major lines of action: grass-roots presence and involvement among very poor families and communities, in housing estates, slums and isolated shanty towns; research into poverty undertaken with the people concerned; and campaigning and mobilising public opinion at local, national and international levels. It is committed to representing people living in extreme poverty at an international level. It aims to unite the experience and knowledge gained from people living in extreme poverty through its numerous grass-roots projects with the academic-based knowledge of various international institutions.

Caritas Social Action Network (CSAN)

CSAN is the official agency of the Catholic Bishops' Conference of England and Wales for domestic social action. It is a family of social action charities which works for the most vulnerable people in society, providing support for families and children, the elderly, the homeless, refugees, the disabled, and prisoners. It works to strengthen and facilitate the network, conduct policy and advocacy work and use its 'voice' at a national level. It is a member of Caritas Internationalis, within the Caritas Europa Group. Caritas holds and promotes a vision of a common humanity, where every person is valuable and valued. Based on Catholic Social Teaching it values the dignity of each individual and strives to provide heartfelt care, justice and universality in its approach to service users and professionalism as a network of charitable organisations.

Catholic Association for Racial Justice (CARJ)

CARJ tackles racial discrimination within the Church and within society. It works to ensure that racial inequality and the racism that causes it are eradicated. It does this through raising awareness of the issues; running training groups in parishes and dioceses; outreach to ethnic minority communities, including Gypsies and Travellers; countering political extremism working with other Church denominations; and supporting Black and Minority Ethnic students so that they realise their potential.

Child Poverty Action Group (CPAG)
CPAG is the leading national charity working to end poverty among children, young people and families in the UK. Its vision is of a society free of child poverty where all children can enjoy their childhoods and have fair chances in life to reach their full potential. It aims to fulfil this vision by being strategic, raising awareness of the causes, extent and impact of child poverty and by advocating strategies for its eradication and prevention; by influencing policy through authoritative, high quality policy work, research and communications and through coalitions and partnerships; through the expertise of its definitive and market-leading welfare benefits publications to maximise family incomes, and through advice, test cases and training providing expert support for frontline advisors on all aspects of social security and tax credit legislation; and offering an informed voice, bringing about positive change for children and families in poverty and ensuring that the needs and entitlements of children and families are voiced and heard globally.

Church Action on Poverty (CAP)
CAP is a national ecumenical Christian social justice charity, committed to tackling poverty in the UK. It works in partnership with churches and with people in poverty themselves to find solutions to poverty, locally, nationally and globally. It aims to build partnerships of hope and transformation based on its values of justice, a belief in freedom from oppression, equality, hope for a better and fairer world; a belief in our common humanity, all made in the image of God so that all people have an intrinsic equal value. It believes in inclusivity, respect and care for others, and responsibility. It affirms people's power to generate solutions to the problems they face, having their own voice, ownership and power, and a right to learning. It believes in speaking the truth to power, in naming, fighting and

challenging injustice, being prophetic and holding power accountable. It believes in active listening, establishing trust and valuing people's unique contribution and voice. It believes in long-term commitment to communities, going the extra mile and seeing it through to seeing change happening.

Citizen Organising Foundation (COF)

COF is a registered charity in the UK whose mission is to create a network of competent, informed and organised citizens who act responsibly in the public life of their communities and are able to influence, for the common good, decisions which impact on their communities. To achieve its mission COF has established an Institute that runs regular training seminars for community leaders and seeks professional organisers to help build broad-based citizen's organisations (BBOs). One well known network is London Citizens which is an alliance of community organisations, largely composed of faith groups including churches and mosques, schools, student organisations, union branches and residents' associations. Among its high profile campaigns was one to establish a living wage and a campaign calling on the Government to regulate the status of illegal immigrants who can prove they have proficiency in English, community ties and no criminal record by offering them permission to stay in the UK legally for two years, with the possibility of citizenship in the end.

Joseph Rowntree Foundation (JRF)

The JRF wants lasting change for people and places in poverty, communities where everyone can thrive and a more equal society, both now and for future generations. Its aim is to identify the root causes of poverty and injustice. In a time of globalisation, economic strain and austerity, the poorer members of our society are at greatest risk. But poverty is not just about money. JRF wants to understand both how much money does matter and what other factors affect equality – housing, education, aspirations, culture. It will search for practical ways to reduce both poverty and wider social and economic inequalities. It also aims to support resilient communities where people thrive and what kind of housing suits different households and different stages of life. It also aims to respond positively to the opportunities and challenges of an ageing society – relationships, money, work, housing, benefits, health, social care, media, technology and design.

Housing Justice
Housing Justice is a charity formed in 2003 when the Catholic Housing Aid Society (CHAS), founded in 1956, and the Churches' National Housing Coalition (CNHC), founded in 1991, merged. It has close links with the churches in England and Wales and works with them on church-based projects to raise the profile of homelessness amongst Christians of all denominations. It is active in over 35 communities across the UK funding housing advice centres, community regeneration projects and supporting church-based homelessness projects. As well as providing practical help to homeless people, it also campaigns against homelessness, lobbying politicians as appropriate. Its predecessor was involved in setting up the All-Party Parliamentary Group on Homelessness and Housing Need in Parliament in 1989. It believes that human dignity is challenged by the lack of a decent home and aims to mobilise Christians to work with and for homeless and badly housed people, the poor and the marginalised.

Shelter
Shelter aims to help people in housing need by supporting families, offering active advice and support, and put the housing crisis back on the national agenda. It aims to be approachable and a lifeline to anyone who is homeless or suffering from bad housing. It believes that home is a basic human need and challenges people in power to make that vision a reality by tenacious lobbying, persuasive research and policy reports, and high-profile public campaigns.

Trussell Trust

The Trussell Trust is a Christian organisation motivated by Jesus' teaching on poverty and injustice. It operates according to Christian principles of compassion, honesty, integrity, openness, kindness and care of all people, regardless of backgrounds or beliefs. It believes in turning faith into practical action, living out God's love for the poor. It is non-judgemental and inclusive, providing assistance to people of all backgrounds and all faiths or none who are found to be in genuine need. It started in 1996 with street babies in Bulgaria and the Trust was founded in 1997 when it began to expand in the UK. In 2000 attention was drawn to the fact that significant numbers of local people faced short-term hunger as a result of a sudden crisis. In 2004 the UK foodbank network was launched teaching churches and communities nationwide how to start their own foodbank. It works to empower local communities to combat poverty and exclusion in the UK and Bulgaria. It works with people that society forgets, providing practical help through sustainable projects and enabling each person to realise they are valued. Its vision is to build communities where people of all backgrounds are included and have the opportunity to live in dignity with hope for the future.

(e) Environmental Sustainability

Christian Ecology Link (CEL)

CEL offers insights into ecology and the environment to Christian people and churches and Christian insights to the Green movement. It believes we are responsible for our impact on God's creation as a whole and it helps members to understand and relate these responsibilities to their faith and encourage others to think seriously about these issues. Its LOAF campaign encourages locally produced, organically grown, animal friendly and fairly traded food. In 2001 it founded Operation Noah which later became a joint project with the Environmental Issues Network of Churches Together in Britain and Ireland. This challenges the Church to realise that care for God's creation and concern about climate change is foundational in the Christian gospel and central to the church's mission.

Friends of the Earth (FOE)
FOE has built up a reputation for successful environmental campaigning over the past 40 years. It recognises that we depend on the planet so aims to keep it healthy and in good shape. It encourages a positive relationship with the environment, acting together for the planet and everyone who lives on it. It aims to wake up the world to climate change, promote laws which protect the countryside, work for better food and cleaner water, and persuade big companies to behave more responsibly. It aims to unite, inspire and empower people to take urgent action necessary to protect the environment for current and future generations by working with others and campaigning to mobilise public support for fair solutions to environmental problems.

Greenpeace
Greeenpeace is a non-governmental environment organisation in over forty countries with an international coordinating body in Holland. Its stated goal is to ensure the ability of the Earth to nurture life in all its diversity. It campaigns on worldwide issues such as global warming, deforestation, overfishing, commercial whaling, genetic engineering and anti-nuclear issues. It uses direct action, lobbying and research to achieve its goals. It evolved from the peace movement and anti-nuclear protests in the late 1960s. It is the most visible environmental organisation in the world. Its direct action strategies have raised environmental issues to public knowledge but are controversial and have sparked legal actions against activists.

International Institute for Environment and Development (IIED)
IIED was founded in 1971 and is one of the world's most influential development and environment policy research

organisations. It works with partners in five continents and promotes the cause of sustainable development. It builds bridges between policy and practice, rich and poor communities, the government and private sector and across diverse interest groups. It contributes to many international policy processes and frameworks.

(f) Authentic Develoment

Catholic Agency for Overseas Development (CAFOD)

CAFOD was founded in 1960 and is the official Catholic aid agency for England and Wales. It works with more than 500 partners overseas, with partners in the UK, and with people of all faiths or none, all working to reduce poverty, wherever the need is greatest. It strives to bring hope, compassion and solidarity to poor communities, standing side by side with them to end poverty and injustice. Inspired by Scripture and Catholic Social Teaching, and the experiences and hopes of people living in poverty, CAFOD works for a safe, sustainable and peaceful world. Comparable organisations include the Scottish Catholic International Aid Fund (SCIAF) and Trócaire in Ireland.

Christian Aid

Christian Aid is a Christian organisation that insists the world can and must be swiftly changed to one where everyone can live a full life, free from poverty. It regards poverty as an outrage against humanity which robs people of dignity, freedom and hope, and power over their own lives. It works globally for profound change that eradicates the causes of poverty, striving to achieve equality, dignity and freedom for all, regardless of faith or nationality. It is part of a wider movement for social justice. It provides urgent, practical and effective assistance where need is great, tackling the effects of poverty as well as its root causes. Its essential purpose is to expose the scandal of poverty, to help in practical ways to root it out from the world, and to challenge and change structures and systems that favour the rich and powerful over the poor and marginalised.

Intermediate Technology Development Group (ITDG)
The ITDG is a non-governmental agency which provides technical assistance in Kenya, Sudan, Zimbabwe, Bangladesh, Sri Lanka, Nepal and Peru. It works towards a more equitable and just world in which technology enriches and benefits the lives of poor people.

Médecins Sans Frontières (MSF)
MSF (Doctors without Borders) is an association made up mainly of doctors and health sector workers. It was officially created in 1971 with the belief that all people have the right to medical care regardless of gender, race, religion, creed or political affiliation, and that the needs of these people outweigh respect for national boundaries. Since its founding it has treated over 100 million patients and now works in over 60 countries around the world with teams ready for any new emergency. It remains fiercely independent of all political, economic or religious powers.

Oxfam
Founded in 1942 Oxfam is an international confederation of 17 organisations working in around 90 countries worldwide to find solutions to poverty and related injustices around the world. Its ultimate goal is to enable people to exercise their rights and manage their own lives. It works directly with communities and seeks to influence the powerful, to ensure that poor people can improve their lives and livelihoods and have a say in decisions that affect them. Each Affiliate works together internationally to achieve a greater impact through collective efforts. Oxfam's programmes address the structural causes of poverty. It assists in the development of structures which directly benefit people facing the realities of poverty and injustice. It recognises the universality and indivisibility of the human rights to a sustainable livelihood, to basic social services, to life and security, to be heard, and to an identity.

Progressio (formerly the Catholic Institute for International Relations, CIIR)
Created in 1940 as the Sword of the Spirit, and in 1965 as the Catholic Institute for International Relations (CIIR), in 2006 it changed its name to Progressio. It is an international development charity that enables poor communities to solve their own problems through support from skilled workers. Throughout its history it has attempted to influence decision-makers, both secular and religious, to support liberation movements and to guard against human rights abuses. It also lobbies legislators to change policies that keep people poor. It works with partner organisations in 11 countries in Latin America, Africa, the Middle East and Asia, combining skill sharing and advocacy in seeking to change systems and practices that create and perpetuate poverty in the global South.

Save the Children
The Save the Children Fund was set up in 1919 to raise funds to provide relief to children suffering the effects of war. It works in more than 120 countries, including the UK, and its vital work reaches more than 80 million children each year through its health and hunger work. It runs world-class programmes to save children's lives and challenges world leaders to keep their promises to give children a brighter future. They are fighting to end the scandal of hunger which is a death sentence for children. It also campaigns against child poverty, for their protection, and for their health and education rights.

WaterAid
WaterAid, which was established as a charitable trust in 1981, is an international non-governmental organisation whose mission is to transform lives by improving access to safe water and improved hygiene and sanitation in the world's poorest communities. It combats the diseases caused by dirty water and poor sanitation which are the second biggest killers of children under five worldwide. It believes that clean water

and safe sanitation underpin health, education and livelihoods. It works with local partners and delivers services, influences decision-makers to make change happen, and generates support across the world.

World Development Movement

The WDM, formed in 1970, is a membership organisation which campaigns on issues of global justice and development in the Global South. It aims to secure important policy changes at national, European and international levels with regard particularly to water justice issues, and the conditions attached by the International Monetary Fund and World Bank to debt relief. It aims to enhance, enlarge and inform the global justice movement through strengthening links between the UK and developing countries and to raise public awareness in the UK of the need for fundamental change from individuals to supranational institutions. It has a network of local groups as well as individual members and it participates in international networks on trade and corporate globalisation and the World Social Forum.

(g) War And Peace

Campaign Against the Arms Trade (CAAT)

CAAT, founded in 1974, is a broad coalition of peace groups and a campaigning organisation working towards the abolition of the international arms trade which it believes has a devastating impact on human rights and security and damages economic development. It also believes that large scale military procurement and arms exports only reinforce a militaristic approach to international problems. In seeking to end the arms trade, CAAT's priorities are to stop the procurement or export of arms where they might exacerbate conflict, support aggression, or increase tension, support an oppressive regime or undermine democracy, or threaten social welfare through high levels of military spending. It aims to end all government political and financial support for arms exports and promote progressive demilitarisation within arms-producing countries.

Campaign for Nuclear Disarmament (CND)

Building on the work of earlier anti-war movements, CND was launched in 1958. It campaigns non-violently to rid the world of nuclear weapons of mass destruction and to create genuine security for future generations. Although its main focus is the scrapping of Trident it also rejects war as a means of solving complex problems and advocates solutions based on dialogue and justice. It campaigns for a global ban on nuclear weapons. CND campaigns both inside and outside parliament, working with allies and supporters within the trade union movement, faith communities and civil society as a whole.

Movement for the Abolition of War (MAW)

MAW believes that war is not inevitable and that we have all the potential tools, skills and laws needed to abolish war. It aims to spread the belief that the abolition of war is both desirable and possible, raise awareness of constructive alternatives to war for resolving national and international disputes, and develop materials and strategies to educate and inform, and to work with others who share their vision.

Pax Christ

Pax Christi is a gospel-based, lay-inspired, peacemaking movement founded in the Catholic Church. Its membership is open to individuals, groups and organisations of all faiths who are in sympathy with its aims. It strives to help the Church and the wider community to proclaim and to make peace, through its experience and ideas, and especially through the witness and action of its members. Its three major objects are: reconciliation; the promotion of a culture of peace and non-violence; and providing the means to bring about peace through peace education, resources and training. It is affiliated to Pax Christi International which is a non-governmental Catholic peace movement working on a global scale on a wide variety of issues in the fields of human rights, human security, disarmament, demilitarisation, just world order, religion and violent conflict.

United Nations Association (UNA-UK)
UNA-UK is the UK's leading source of independent analysis on the UN, and a UK-wide grassroots movement. It believes that a strong, credible and effective UN is essential if we are to build a safer, fairer and more sustainable world. It advocates strong government support for the UN and demonstrates why the UN matters to people everywhere. It pursues its mission by connecting people to the work and values of the UN; influencing decision-makers and opinion-shapers to support UN goals; explaining how the UN works and what it can realistically achieve; stimulating debate and action on how to make the UN more effective; and equipping its members and supporters to further all of these aims.

4. Concluding Reflections

So we come to the end of my letters to you about what you are called to do as a follower of Jesus to tackle the injustices and inequalities which are to be found not only in our own society but also throughout the whole world. To recap: In Part I I offered an outline of the world as it is both in this country, domestically, and internationally. In Part II I suggested an explanation for the social reality and the structural causes of the injustices. In Part III I outlined some Christian responses in terms of Scripture and Catholic Social Teaching and in this final Part IV I have outlined some ways in which you might respond and indicated some of the resources which would be helpful to you. In this final letter I have suggested that as a follower of Jesus an appropriate place to start might be your own parish justice and peace group. I also argued that involvement in local and national politics is an important calling and well-worth your consideration. Finally, I have provided brief outlines of some of the many campaigning groups in specific areas. If you have a particular concern, whether human rights, homelessness, development or the arms trade, you would find it useful to explore further information about the topic and main campaigning groups.

I would like to end this letter with a quotation from a well-known French Protestant pastor that I came across recently. He wrote the following as a letter from God having listened to our prayers for people in distress:

'Dear children,

'It seems to me you've plenty of cheek! You ask me to undertake what is in fact your own responsibility. It really is a bit much!

'You are asking me to establish justice and peace in the world, to take care of the sick, to come to the aid of those being tortured, to provide daily bread (and clean water) to the hungry, to give a good heart to children and young people, generosity and serenity to the aged, courage and a firm will to politicians, to set prisoners free, to bring exiles home... and plenty more of a similar nature...

'But that is what you are there for, the mission which I have entrusted to you! It's up to you to consider and then to act... If I have properly understood your theories of the origins of humanity... I am supposed to have given you: a large brain (which you often don't bother to use), a compassionate heart, an enterprising spirit, a sensitivity to human suffering, hands and arms to get to work with, and everything else... so what do you do with them? And then you ask me to intervene?

'In my great wisdom I am fully aware that all these requests are inspired by worthy sentiments and good intentions... but you well know that these are not enough. Indeed, you even say that the way to hell is paved with them. (I am not sure what you are calling 'hell' unless you mean the mess you are making of the planet.)

'Anyway, I'm always sending you prophets to remind you... and what do you do? You suppress them! Get on with it. Please! Each of you, have a smidgeon of spiritual courage!'

I couldn't have put it better! I do hope that you will be encouraged to 'get on with it', make a start yourselves and help make this lovely world that God has given us a better and more just place for us all to live in.

* 9 7 8 1 7 8 4 5 6 0 1 5 7 *

ND - #0176 - 060826 - C0 - 216/138/16 - PB - 9781784560157 - Gloss Lamination